Praise for Mom, Across The Miles

In this profound work, Vivek Sinha masterfully weaves personal narrative with universal leadership lessons drawn from the enduring wisdom of his late mother. Mom, Across the Miles is more than a tribute; it is an instructive guide for readers seeking to lead with empathy, resilience, and purpose. The insights imparted through his mother's teachings transcend cultural and generational boundaries, offering timeless principles that readers can apply to their own personal growth and professional leadership journeys.

– Danielle Hansen
President, Strategic Training Endeavors;
Clinical Professor, University of St. Thomas

True leadership starts with listening, and few people capture that better than Vivek Sinha in this heartfelt tribute. His mother's lessons, born from everyday conversations, offer powerful insights into how empathy, resilience, and curiosity can shape a leader's journey.

–Geoff Martha,
Chairman & CEO, Medtronic

A beautiful reflection of one mother's intentional approach to teach her son life lessons and skills that have taken him far only because he listened and applied them thoughtfully over the years both personally and professionally.

– Greg Wetzel
Head of Global Service Parts Planning, GE HealthCare

"Mom, Across the Miles is a beautiful and inspiring tribute to the power of a mother's love. With warmth and wisdom, it reminds us that a mother's influence transcends distance, time, and culture–shaping who we are and who we become. This book speaks to the heart of every reader, no matter where they come from, offering both comfort and inspiration. It also reminded me of my own mother's wisdom and love, which continue to shape the person I am today and inspire me to be the best mother I can for my own children. A truly universal celebration of the bond between mothers and children."

– Jennifer Kirk

Chief Executive Officer, Exubrion Therapeutics
Independent Director - Sempra (SRE), Republic Services (RSG)

""Mom Across the Miles" is a moving tribute to the quiet strength of motherhood, written with tenderness, reflection, and deep emotional honesty. Vivek Sinha beautifully captures what so many of us feel but often struggle to express – the complex, enduring bond between a mother and son, stretched across years and continents.

What touched me most is the book's humility. It doesn't shout; it resonates. And through its pages, we're reminded that true gratitude lies not in grand gestures, but in small moments of understanding, care, and reflection.

As someone who has long believed in leading with empathy and honoring personal roots, I found this memoir deeply meaningful. Vivek's storytelling is as graceful as it is grounded – a quality that makes this book a heartfelt read for anyone navigating family, migration, or the emotional distance success sometimes brings.

I hope many discover this quiet gem. It's a timely reminder that no matter how far we travel, some bonds travel with us – always."

– K.B. Kachru

Chairman – South Asia, Radisson Hotel Group.
Author, Humility and Agility: The Life of a Hotelier

"Through deeply personal stories, Vivek Sinha shows that some of life's most profound leadership lessons come not from classrooms or boardrooms, but from the unconditional love and wisdom of a mother. This book is both a touching tribute and an inspiring guide for leaders navigating complexity with grace and humanity."

– Karen Parkhill
EVP & Chief Financial Officer, HP Inc.

"Mom, Across the Miles is a moving tribute to maternal wisdom and its quiet yet profound influence on our lives and leadership. Through deeply personal stories and timeless cultural reflections, Vivek Sinha captures the soul of a mother's love–patient, resilient, and transformative. This book is both a heartfelt memoir and a powerful guide for leading with empathy, purpose, and grace."

– MR Rangaswami
Founder Indiaspora

"Mom, Across the Miles is a powerful meditation on love, loss, and legacy. As a Hindu, I found Vivek Sinha's reflections especially relatable – the references to the seven forms of the mother from the Bhagavata Purana, the dharmic values, and the interweaving of cultural identity with personal growth struck a deep chord. This book is a gift to anyone reflecting on their own relationship with a parent or the enduring influence of a mother's quiet strength. A moving blend of heart and philosophy that lingers long after the last page."

– Padma Kuppa

CIO, Project DIAMOnD | Writer & Consultant

"Mom, Across the Miles is a genuine and touching tribute to a mother's quiet strength. Through personal stories and thoughtful reflections, Vivek Sinha highlights how the lessons learned at home–love, resilience, and empathy–shape the way we lead and support others.

It's a reminder that leadership often begins in everyday moments, and that the values passed down through generations can guide us in both life and work."

– Rashmi Kumar

CIO, Medtronic

"A heartfelt tribute to a mother's quiet strength, Mom, Across the Miles is both memoir and meditation. With warmth and insight, Vivek Sinha shows us how our mothers shape us gently throughout our lives with lessons on leadership, resilience, and purpose. A deeply moving reminder, too, that some of life's most powerful lessons begin with a simple phone call."

– Srilata Zaheer

Professor and Elmer L. Andersen Chair in Global CSR, Carlson School of Management, University of Minnesota

"In Mom, Across the Miles, Vivek Sinha masterfully bridges the personal and the universal through the lens of his relationship with his mother. As an oral historian, I'm struck by the tenderness and clarity with which he honors intergenerational wisdom and cultural identity. This book is a heartfelt tribute to the enduring power of love, memory, and leadership rooted in compassion."

– Tea Rozman

Oral Historian and Co-Founder and Co-Executive Director, Green Card Voices

““Mom, Across The Miles” by Vivek Sinha is a delightful reflection on a mother and son’s love for each other, parental wisdom, a rich multi-cultural past, the archetype of motherhood, connectedness and longing, and the relevance of motherly values in leadership roles. The beautiful writing evoked vivid memories from my own parental relationship, laughter, and tears, and added depth to my appreciation of the mothers in my life.”

– Tom Savard

Sr. Director, R&D. Medtronic Inc.

Author of The Clarity Cascade: Unleashing Hidden Value to Accelerate Product Development and Multiply ROI

सुबोध कांत सहाय
SUBODH KANT SAHAI
Former Union Minister
Government of India

19th July, 2025

Dear Vivek

It is both a privilege and a personal honor to write this foreword for *Mom, Across the Miles: Life & Leadership Lessons – One Call at a Time. A* work that transcends being just a book. It is a heartfelt reflection on love, resilience, and the quiet yet profound leadership of a mother who shaped lives in ways words can only begin to capture.

Pushpa (Verma) Sinha, whom I proudly called my cousin sister-in-law "Bhabhi", embodied grace, selflessness, and strength. As someone who witnessed her journey closely, I can say with certainty that she carried the weight of responsibility not as a burden, but as a quiet commitment to those she loved. She was the unshakable center of her family, offering stability and wisdom in every season of life.

How a man completely depends on his wife my brother "Suman Bhai" is an example and my Bhabhi used to take care of him from morning till night despite living in a joint family and the approach of Pushpa Bhabhi was always reflecting motherly.

Vivek's reflections in this book are drawn from real moments, shared over long-distance phone calls, across continents, and over years. These conversations weren't just updates on life; they were acts of connection, love, and growth. Through them, he absorbed his mother's values, learned how to lead with empathy, and preserved a bond that not even time or distance could weaken.

What touched me most is how this book captures the spirit of motherhood not as a role, but as a legacy. Pushpa ji's influence echoes throughout Vivek's life—not only in how he leads his family and career, but in how he continues to ask deeper questions, seek wisdom, and nurture others.

Add:- 100, South Avenue, New Delhi-110011
Tel: +91-11-23018317, 23018318/ E-mail: subodhkant.sahai@gov.in

सुबोध कांत सहाय
SUBODH KANT SAHAI
Former Union Minister
Government of India

As someone who has spent a lifetime in public service, I can say this with conviction: the most lasting leadership is often forged in the private, unseen spaces of life. This book affirms that truth. It invites readers to pause, reflect, and reconnect with the voices and values that shaped them.

Vivek's work here is not simply a remembrance. It is a contribution, a bridge between generations, cultures, and hearts. I commend him for capturing something so intimate, yet so universally resonant. *Mom, Across the Miles* is a gift to anyone who cherishes the quiet strength of family and the timeless imprint of a mother's guidance.

With regards,

(SUBODH KANT SAHAY)

Add:- 100, South Avenue, New Delhi-110011
Tel: +91-11-23018317, 23018318/ E-mail: subodhkant.sahai@gov.in

Mom, Across The Miles

Life & Leadership Lessons - One Call At A Time

Vivek Sinha

Become Shakespeare .com

First Published in 2025

Becomeshakespeare.com

One Point Six Technologies Pvt Ltd

Unit no. 26, Ground Floor,
A1, Shram Safalya,
Wadala Truck Terminal Road,
Near Post Office, Antop Hill, M
umbai - 400037

T: +91 8080226699

ISBN - 978-93-6263-238-8

Dedication

To my beloved mother, **Late Puspha (Verma) Sinha**, whose wisdom, strength, and love nurtured all who knew her.

This book stands as a testament to her legacy—rooted in her lessons, shaped by her spirit, and dedicated to the nurturers of the world.

Born of her care, guided by her wisdom, and devoted to her memory.

This book is

of the nurturer, by the nurturer, for the nurturer.

Acknowledgments

This book would not have been possible without the unwavering support of my family.

My wife, **Shilpi Sinha**, has been my greatest pillar. Her remarkable ability to give me the space and time I needed made every word of this book possible. Without that quiet strength, I couldn't have written a single line.

Our two teenage children have also played an invaluable role. **Anushkaa Sinha**, with her sharp eye for detail and honest critiques, has been an exceptional proofreader—ensuring that my writing is clear and compelling. **Arnav Sinha**, with his creative input on the cover design and his thought-provoking questions, has pushed me to refine my ideas beyond what I thought possible. Their contributions go beyond gratitude.

A special mention must go to **Ms. Greta Huttanus**, the editor and motivator behind this book. She runs Open Voices at Open Book Minneapolis, a nonprofit club for authors that has been instrumental in shaping this work. Her guidance has been invaluable.

Heartfelt gratitude to my father, **Dr. Binay Kumar Sinha**, and my sisters & brother-in-laws, **Dr. Archana Sinha** & **Sanjay P Sinha** and **Anumeha Bardaiyar** & **Rohit Bardaiyar** for their invaluable life lessons, unwavering support, and constant guidance that have shaped my journey.

With full transparency, I also want to acknowledge the role of technology in bringing this book to life. Research tools like Google, and writing assistants such as ChatGPT, Gemini, and Grammarly, have helped me refine my thoughts and transform them into structured words. As someone who does not consider himself an author, these tools have been essential in making this book a reality.

To each and every person and resource that have contributed to this journey, thank you. This book is a product of collaboration, learning, and unwavering support.

"I may have written this book with my name on the cover, but parts of it were emotionally edited by people who know me better than I know myself."

Meet Altamash, Sarwesh, Sanjeev, Sudhanshu, Vikas, and Vimal—alphabetically arranged not because they'd argue about the order (which they absolutely would), but because even in chaos, there is some method.

These aren't just my friends. These are the people who've had front-row seats to the unfiltered, unshaven, sometimes unnecessarily philosophical version of me.

They're the ones who can roast me without mercy yet defend me without pause. I trust them with my truth, and my mother—who had an uncanny radar for good people—trusted them with hers.

Testimony

From Dr. Archana Sinha & Anumeha Bardaiyar

"This book is more than just Vivek's story–it's ours too. Through each chapter, he has brought our mother's essence to life: her wisdom, resilience, quiet grace, and boundless love. Reading it felt like sitting beside her again, hearing her gentle voice, her timeless guidance, and her deep faith in all of us.

She was our center–anchoring the family with strength and warmth–and this book captures that beautifully. It's a tribute not just to the mother we knew, but to the values she instilled in us, the lives she touched, and the legacy she left behind. We're proud of Vivek for honoring her in such a moving, meaningful way."

– **Dr. Archana Sinha** and **Anumeha Bardaiyar**
Vivek's sisters and proud daughters of Pushpa (Verma) Sinha

From My Brothers From Other Mothers

We've known Vivek since the days of cricket in the gullies, school tiffins swapped under banyan trees, and epic debates that ended only when someone's mom called us home. This book isn't just his story—it's ours too.

It's the story of a son shaped by a mother whose quiet strength influenced all of us. Some of us are second-generation friends, meaning our parents knew his parents—and that legacy of connection runs deep.

Reading *Mom, Across The Miles* felt like listening to one of our old conversations—equal parts wisdom, humor, and heart. It's a tribute not just to one incredible mother, but to all mothers who raise not just their own children, but whole communities.

We saw these moments unfold. We lived some of them with him. And now, we couldn't be prouder to see them bound between these pages.

Altamash, Sarwesh, Sanjeev, Sudhanshu, Vikas, and Vimal

The Goal

The goal of this book isn't just to share my experiences; it's to spark reflection on the lessons and the wisdom your own parents have passed down to you.

These stories aren't meant to sit in the corner of your personal life; they are meant to flow into your professional world, because life and work aren't two separate spheres to balance; they're threads of the same fabric.

If, at any moment while reading, you find yourself smiling or thinking, "*This feels familiar... this reminds me of my own life*," then I know I've done what I set out to do.

Contents

Introduction	1
Prologue	9
Mother - The Horizon	15
Chapter I: Unconditional Love	37
Chapter II: Equality	59
Chapter III: A Reflection Of Maya	95
Chapter IV: Respect	123
Chapter V: Nurture The Resources	147
Chapter VI: A Nurse	173
Chapter VII: The Embodiment Of Tolerance	195
Beyond The Horizon	217

Introduction

I was born and raised in Gaya, a small town in the Indian state of Bihar, better known internationally as the site of Buddha's enlightenment and the birthplace of Buddhism.

If I had been born today, I would almost certainly have been diagnosed with mild dyslexia. It's not that we had scarcity of resources and/or education. Fortunately, we had an abundance of resources, although the definition was very different for me while growing up. Unawareness of dyslexia, or, say, ignoring dyslexia was mainly due to the "Living in and with the flow of life".

I grew up in a joint family, a traditional Indian household arrangement where multiple generations, grandparents, uncles, aunts, cousins, and their children live under the same roof, sharing not just space but responsibilities, values, and lives.

It's a social structure rooted in the idea of collectivism over individualism. While the nuclear family emphasizes independence, a joint family thrives on interdependence. Financial responsibilities are often pooled, and decision-making tends to be collective, typically guided by the senior-most male member, or *karta*, of the family.

The eldest of the four brothers who lived and worked in Gaya under the same ancestral roof was my father. He was the second oldest among six siblings and stepped into the role of the family's symbolic leader after our grandfather passed away in the early 1980s. Our home was always full—with parents, uncles, aunts, and cousins living together in a shared rhythm of daily life. Every member had a defined role and a set of responsibilities, often shaped by tradition and seniority.

Although growing up in such a setting came with its challenges—conflicting priorities, generational differences, and a lack of privacy—it also provided a deep sense of belonging and support. Unquestionably, it was a happy home.

My father, a chemistry professor at the local university, enjoyed a flexible work schedule. He was an extremely outgoing person who cherished his time with long-time childhood friends and took part in a wide range of sports including bridge, cricket, badminton, tennis, and table tennis.

His strong social life, however, came at a cost to my mother. Her responsibilities were numerous and layered—those of a wife, a mother, the *bari bahu* (eldest daughter-in-law), and *bhabhi* (sister-in-law). In a joint family, the eldest daughter-in-law often serves as the central figure managing the household's day-to-day dynamics, which can be both an honor and a burden.

Culturally, in many such families, a father is expected to become a more prominent figure in a son's life only later in boyhood—once the child is grown enough to understand discipline and expectations. In the early years, nurturing often falls primarily to the mother. The interaction between father and son tends to be functional, limited to basic daily exchanges. Over time, this social construct can unintentionally create a psychological distance between father and child.

In my case, this distance became a defining part of my upbringing, and paradoxically, it helped me forge an even deeper bond with my mother. She was my constant—emotionally accessible, always present, and deeply invested in my day-to-day life.

In our joint family, success was primarily measured by academic performance—specifically, by grades and class rankings. This emphasis stemmed from the family's strong academic legacy: all of my uncles held either a master's degree or a Ph.D., and my aunts were at least undergraduate degree holders, with some even pursuing their master's after marriage.

Academic achievement was closely tied to one's social standing and the family's reputation within the community. As children, we were constantly reminded of the importance of doing well in school—not just for our own future, but to uphold the family's name. There was an unspoken expectation that we should not only succeed but also outperform our cousins and peers.

Looking back, I can now clearly recognize that I had dyslexia, based on the symptoms I experienced and the way I processed information. Reading and writing were especially challenging for me. I struggled with grammar, spelling, and comprehension, and learning a new language like English was even harder because I had difficulty distinguishing the sounds that letters make.

At the time, I didn't know I was dyslexic—but not knowing it didn't hold me back. In fact, it shaped my perspective in a powerful way. I learned early on to focus on developing my strengths rather than becoming consumed by my weaknesses.

As Peter Drucker, a renowned management thinker, once said, "*A person can perform only from strength. One cannot build performance on weakness.*" In many ways, I am a poster example of that belief. No one is perfect—and that realization became a source of resilience rather than limitation.

Although I was born healthy, I didn't utter a single word until I was two and a half years old. While this isn't necessarily abnormal, it causes significant anxiety within our community. People began to doubt my intellectual abilities, labeling me as *slow* or even *dumb*. These whispered judgments and societal pressures created a challenging environment for both my mother and me.

Despite growing concerns about my delayed speech, my mother never wavered in her belief in my potential. Over time, I began to speak, though pronouncing certain complex or tongue-twisting words remained a challenge, even to this day. While some saw this as a shortcoming, it became an unexpected strength. It taught me to express my thoughts and emotions with clarity, brevity, and intention choosing meaningful words over elaborate ones.

Not being able to articulate every word somehow heightened my ability to sense people's feelings and reactions without waiting for them to speak. At times, I've wondered whether I fit the definition of *disabled*, especially when I look at how various governments classify disabilities. By those standards, I might be considered one, but if we follow that logic, wouldn't everyone be disabled in some way? I refuse to see myself as disabled. In fact, I consider myself more capable, with an IQ undoubtedly above the average person.

What others viewed as a limitation, I now recognize as a gift, one that has shaped how I understand and connect with the world.

Being bilingual is regarded as a mark of intelligence and success in my society. But for me, it was just another hurdle to overcome. I constantly felt like I was playing catch-up, and I worried about how my peers and family perceived me. I struggled throughout elementary school and often believed I would never succeed academically–that I was somehow a failure.

However, my mother never gave up on me. She gave me the confidence to keep going and helped me find resources to support my learning challenges. With her encouragement and guidance, I gradually improved my reading and writing skills. I also began to understand how to manage and even leverage my dyslexia. By high school, I was doing well, and eventually, I made it to college.

Without the unwavering support of my family and the resources they pointed me toward, I wouldn't be where I am today. Dyslexia, in hindsight, has strengthened and shaped my character. It taught me to persevere and to approach problems with creativity.

Today, I hold two master's degrees—one from a prestigious institution in India and another from a renowned university in the USA. I now lead strategic initiatives in a global organization, working at the intersection of business and innovation. These academic and professional accomplishments, along with the joy of a loving and supportive family, affirm my belief that I am on a meaningful path to success.

I'm grateful for the opportunities that have shaped my journey and remain committed to the continued pursuit of excellence. Even with a learning disability, success in school and in life is entirely possible. Just remember: never give up on yourself, and always seek the support you need.

Prologue

In the chapters that follow, I delve into the intricacies of my relationship with my mother, largely sustained across continents through long-distance phone calls. This narrative unfolds against the backdrop of my relocation to Minneapolis, Minnesota, USA, in 2007. A move prompted by career aspirations that ultimately reshaped the dynamics of our connection.

Minneapolis became my home city defined by its stark winters, where temperatures often plummet well below zero, painting the landscape with a relentless frost. The state of Minnesota, affectionately known as the *Land of 10,000 Lakes*, boasts over 14,000 sparkling bodies of water, each covering at least ten acres. These lakes, nestled amidst dense forests and sprawling countryside, give the region a unique charm.

Minneapolis itself is a vibrant hub of culture and commerce, renowned for its strong educational institutions, world-class medical facilities, and a thriving corporate presence that includes some of the globe's most prominent companies. Among these, my employer played a pivotal role in my journey, intertwining my professional aspirations with the city's opportunities.

Yet, even amid all the growth, change, and achievement, one constant remained: my mother's belief in me. Her voice—steady, loving, and full of quiet strength—traveled across the miles and reminded me, time and again, to never give up on myself and to always seek the help I needed. She was the reason I kept moving forward.

Our daily ritual of communication became an anchor in the midst of this new chapter in my life. Each weekday morning, during my commute to work, I would call her, timed perfectly to align with the quiet evening hours in India. I later learned from my sister that during this time, my mother deliberately avoided answering any other calls, reserving these moments exclusively for me. This small yet profound gesture reflected the depth of her care and the value she placed on maintaining our bond.

What made these conversations special was their organic flow, no simple "hello" to begin, but rather warm, curious inquiries like, "Tell me...," "What were you doing...," or "What's new...." These words weren't mere pleasantries; they were invitations to share, to connect, and to bridge the physical distance between us.

In those fleeting moments, we weren't just exchanging updates; we were cultivating a relationship, rich with meaning and understanding. Her attention to detail and her unwavering focus during these calls demonstrated how much she valued this connection, a sentiment I reciprocated with equal sincerity.

To describe my mother's role in our family simply as a "housewife" would diminish her profound contributions. She was, in every sense of the word, a homemaker, a title that embodies the essence of her dedication to creating a nurturing and harmonious environment for us all. Beyond managing the physical household, she was the emotional cornerstone of our family, balancing caregiving, organizing, and fostering strong familial bonds with unerring precision. Her role extended far beyond traditional domestic responsibilities; she was the unseen architect of our happiness and stability.

My mother was also an educated woman, holding a Bachelor of Arts degree. She had dreams of pursuing a master's degree, but life, as it often does, had other plans. Her academic aspirations took a backseat with the arrival of her first child, my elder sister. Yet, this pause in formal education did not signify an end to her learning. In fact, her life became her greatest teacher.

Her journey began with hardship. Born into a respected family in Munger, Bihar, her father was a renowned doctor who passed away when she was still a child. This loss could have defined her life with sorrow, but instead, it became the foundation of her resilience. Supported by her elder siblings, she grew up navigating life's challenges with quiet determination. These early trials shaped her into a woman of immense strength, humility, and empathy, qualities that became her hallmark as she guided our family through life's inevitable ups and downs.

Adversity, for her, was not a stumbling block but a crucible that forged her character. She transformed pain into purpose, approaching every challenge with a blend of practicality and inner strength. Her humility was not born from a lack of achievements but from an intimate understanding of life's fragility and the fleeting nature of success. Her empathy, cultivated through her own hardships, allowed her to connect deeply with the struggles and joys of others.

As a mother, she embodied love in its purest, most unconditional form. She sacrificed without hesitation, loved without limits, and guided without imposing. Every moment of her life was a testament to her unwavering commitment to her family. She taught us that true strength lies in vulnerability, that humility is a mark of wisdom, and that love is the most enduring legacy one can leave behind.

Now, as I reflect on our countless conversations, her sacrifices, and the indelible impact she has had on my life, I realize that she was more than just my mother. She was my first teacher, my guiding light, and the foundation upon which I built my life. Through this book, I hope to honor her memory, sharing the lessons she imparted and the love she so selflessly gave.

Her story is not just hers; it is a universal narrative of motherhood, resilience, and the enduring power of love. As you journey through these pages, you will see glimpses of your own mothers, their sacrifices, their wisdom, and their boundless love. For in the story of one mother lies the story of all mothers, a story that transcends time, culture, and boundaries.

Mother - The Horizon

Hindi - Maa
English - Mother, Mama, Mom
Arabic – Umm / Ummi
Asturian - Ma
Belarusan - Matka
Bosnian - Majka
Cambodian - Mæ, Madai, Mák
Danish - Mor
Dutch - Moeder, Moer
Estonian - Ema
French - Mère, Maman
German - Mutter
Greek - Mána
Hawaiian - Makuahine
Latin - Mater
Norwegian – Mor
Persian - Madr, Maman
Romanian - Mama, Maica

Spanish - Madre, MamÃ¡, Mami
Urdu - Ammee
Vietnamese - me

In most languages the alphabet "M" is part of the word, for me *Mother* is synonym of *Miracle.* A mother does miracles for their child.

- An adoptive mother is a female who has legally adopted a kid and is now the child's parent.
- A biological mother is a woman who contributed genetically to the child's genesis through sex or egg donation.
- A putative mother is a woman who has not yet been proven to be the biological mother of a child.
- A stepmother is a woman who is married to a child's parent, and they may form a family unit, but who generally does not have the legal rights and responsibilities of a parent in relation to the child.

There are many other classifications: biological mother, non-biological mother, surrogate mother, lesbian and bisexual motherhood, transgender motherhood, and the list goes on.

The relationship between a mother and her child is hard to put into words.

Motherhood is a biological occurrence that primarily affects women. Motherhood is not just the biological process by which new individuals are produced. It is a psychosocial journey. Every culture has a sociocultural construction.

The role of a mother is highly valued across geography and culture. Here are a few examples that highlight the importance of mothers across different cultures and regions.

In Peruvian culture, mothers have a vital function. In certain households, the mother is the matriarch and serves as the *trunk* of the family tree, the foundation of the home, and a key factor in maintaining the family unit. The indigenous Andean people of Peru also honor *Pachamama*, or Mother Earth, for her gifts. Many native Andean populations revere the old legendary goddess Pachamama. According to mythology, Pachamama is the fertility goddess in charge of planting and harvesting. Her day of adoration is known as Martes de Challa.

In Cambodia, mothers are an important element of the family and the link that binds everyone together. They function as their husbands' advisers as well as the family's caregivers, keepers, and protectors of the home. Many mothers manage the family's finances as well. Women have long been honored in Cambodia, as seen by the comparisons to celestial deities found on the walls of the enormous Angkor Wat temples.

In Vietnam, the mother plays a very important role in the household. Vietnamese society has a strong matriarchal legacy that stretches back to the country's early years, when women frequently assumed leadership roles with minimal local resistance. Strong female leaders throughout Vietnamese history, including Trieu Thi Trinh and the Trung Sisters, were essential to the nation's survival. The legacy these ladies left impacted how Vietnam views the roles that women play in society today.

In many African traditions, mothers hold a central role as life givers, both biologically and spiritually. They are seen as the heart of family and community well-being, nurturing not only their children but the cultural values that bind generations. Ancestors, particularly mothers, are revered through rituals and oral traditions, keeping their legacy alive. African proverbs, such as 'A mother's heart is a child's classroom,' beautifully capture their lasting influence on character and learning, emphasizing their role as the first educators.

Across Native American cultures, the Earth is revered as a nurturing mother, providing sustenance and life for all beings. This deep connection with nature underscores the spiritual and cultural significance of mothers as creators and caregivers. Women, especially mothers, were often community leaders, embodying strength and wisdom, and played pivotal roles in spiritual practices and decision-making. Their influence extended beyond the family, shaping the community's harmony and resilience.

In European history, the concept of motherhood has been celebrated through mythology, religion, and cultural rituals. Ancient Greeks and Romans honored goddesses like Gaia and Cybele, who symbolized maternal strength and the nurturing forces of nature. Celebrations like Matronalia recognized maternal roles in sustaining life and society. During medieval times, the Virgin Mary emerged as a universal icon of maternal compassion and sacrifice. As the mother of Jesus, she epitomized purity and unconditional love, deeply influencing art, literature, and religious devotion across Europe.

In Aotearoa New Zealand, particularly within Māori culture, mothers and maternal figures are deeply respected as the *kaitiaki*–guardians of life, values, and identity. They are often seen as the spiritual backbone of the *whānau* (family), responsible not only for nurturing the body but also for shaping the heart and mind. Through *mātauranga Māori* (traditional knowledge) and *whakataukī* (proverbs), their wisdom is passed down across generations. One such proverb, 'He wahine, he whenua, e ngaro ai te tangata' (By women and land, men are lost), honors the sacred connection between women, land, and survival—underscoring a mother's central role in cultural continuity and collective well-being.

Christianity places significant emphasis on the sacred role of motherhood, viewing it as a divine calling entrusted to women by God. The Bible offers guidance for Christian mothers—such as in Titus 2:4–5, which encourages them to love and care for their children with devotion. This love is seen not only as an expression of maternal care, but also as a way to honor God and reflect the character of the Savior they follow.

The virtues of a godly mother are beautifully illustrated in Proverbs 31:25–28: Strength and dignity are her clothing, and she laughs at the time to come. She opens her mouth with wisdom, and the teaching of kindness is on her tongue. She looks well to the ways of her household and does not eat the bread of idleness. These verses celebrate qualities such as wisdom, kindness, and diligence—portraying a woman of grace, resilience, and unwavering commitment to her family and faith.

Jewish tradition deeply values mothers, emphasizing their crucial role in nurturing children and shaping their Jewish identity. The commandment 'Honor your father and your mother' (Exodus 20:12), a cornerstone of Jewish ethics, underscores the profound respect and care owed to mothers. Mothers are seen as pillars of strength and unwavering love, with their contributions to family and community highly esteemed.

Islam places a great deal of value on mothers. Without a doubt the most cherished relationship and the foundation of all existence is that between a mother and her children. A mother gives birth to a child after carrying it inside of her for nine months, cares for it, and frequently puts the needs of the child above her own. There are various passages in the Quran and Hadith that stress the value of parents, especially mothers. 'Allah has enjoined on man kindness to his parents; in pain did his mother bear him, and in pain, did she give him birth.' (Quran:46:15)

Throughout the ages, mothers have been celebrated as the ultimate bearers of life, often symbolized by goddesses, the Earth, or revered human figures. They embody the essence of creation and nurturing, providing the foundation for life's continuity. The universal narrative of motherhood is deeply intertwined with sacrifice and strength, as mothers across cultures and generations have selflessly endured hardships for the well-being of their children. This enduring story of love and resilience transcends borders and eras, highlighting their pivotal role in human existence.

Mothers are also regarded as moral and spiritual guides, serving as the first educators who shape values and impart wisdom. In many cultures, they are seen as the cornerstone of ethical and emotional development, offering guidance that influences not just families but entire communities. Their nurturing spirit is complemented by their ability to instill a sense of purpose, balance, and respect for life, making them spiritual anchors in the lives of their children.

While traditional roles often emphasize mothers as caregivers, modern societies increasingly recognize their multifaceted identities, celebrating their contributions beyond the household. Whether as professionals, leaders, or nurturers, mothers continue to inspire with their resilience and compassion. In every era, they remain timeless symbols of love and strength, bridging the past, present, and future with their unwavering dedication to life and family.

Across generations, cultures, and religions, the role of a mother has consistently been revered as a divine and natural calling bestowed upon women. This sacred role is not merely a societal construct but is often seen as a profound responsibility given by nature, a higher power, or God, to nurture, shape, and guide the course of life itself.

Mothers are the architects of humanity, entrusted with the task of instilling values, fostering growth, and molding generations to come. As Maya Angelou once eloquently said, *To describe my mother would be to write about a hurricane in its perfect power. Or the climbing, falling colors of a rainbow.* Her words capture the awe-inspiring depth and strength inherent in a mother's role, transcending time and cultural boundaries.

The essence of motherhood is universal, yet its expression is deeply personal and multifaceted. Whether seen through the lens of spirituality, biology, or social responsibility, a mother embodies the enduring connection between the past and the future, carrying the extraordinary power to shape the lives entrusted to her care. It is a role that defines not just families but the very fabric of humanity.

The Bhagavata Purana, one of the principal sacred texts of Hinduism, also referred to as the Srimad Bhagavatam or Srimad Bhagavata Mahapurana, offers profound insights into various aspects of life, spirituality, and relationships. Among its teachings, it beautifully describes the concept of the mother in seven distinct forms, each embodying a unique facet of nurturing, guidance, and sustenance. This depiction transcends the biological role of a mother, emphasizing her as a universal figure of care and creation, which can resonate with readers from any cultural or religious background.

I. The real mother– ātma-mātā

II. The wife of the spiritual master– guroḥ-patnī

III. The wife of a brāhmaṇa– brāhmaṇi

IV. The wife of the king– rāja-patnikā

V. The cow– dhenuḥ

VI. The nurse– dhātrī

VII. The earth– pṛthvī

I. **The Real Mother: A Symbol Of Unconditional Love**

The real mother, or biological mother, is the one who gives birth to a child, a bond forged through the extraordinary journey of nurturing life within her for nine months. This act alone is a testament to her unparalleled selflessness.

While the father plants the seed, it is the mother who creates a sanctuary for that life to grow, providing warmth, sustenance, and safety. Her role doesn't conclude with birth; rather, it marks the beginning of a lifelong commitment. She becomes the child's first teacher, imparting lessons through love, guidance, and protection during the most impressionable years.

A mother's love is not bound by conditions or shaped by recognition. It flows as an enduring force, forgiving and uplifting, even in moments when it is taken for granted. This love is instinctive, limitless, and unwavering, a pure form of devotion that seeks nothing in return. It is through her sacrifices and resilience that the real mother shows the depth of her commitment, embodying a love that stands steadfast in the face of challenges.

The role of a real mother transcends the physical act of giving birth. She is a guardian, a nurturer, and a silent architect of her child's future. Her love is the foundation upon which children build their lives, a reminder that true love is not about what is given or received but about the willingness to give everything selflessly, simply because it is in her nature to do so.

II. The Wife Of The Spiritual Master or Teacher: A Lesson In Equality

In ancient India, or *Bharat*, as it used to be called before the British colonial administration adopted 'India' as the official name– the *Gurukul* system played a pivotal role in education and the holistic development of individuals. Derived from Sanskrit, *guru* meaning 'teacher' or 'master' and *kul* meaning 'family' or 'domain.' The Gurukul was more than a school; it was a place where students lived and learned together, forming an extended familial bond with their teacher and fellow disciples.

Within this system, the wife of the spiritual master, or teacher, held a revered position. She played a vital role in shaping the environment of the Gurukul, ensuring that the students not only acquired knowledge but also internalized values such as humility, discipline, and service. Her nurturing presence complemented the intellectual and moral teachings of the guru, creating a balanced and supportive atmosphere for holistic growth.

Students in Gurukul were treated as equals, irrespective of their social or economic background. They lived together, sharing responsibilities and performing daily chores, including cooking, cleaning, and other menial tasks, alongside their studies. This hands-on experience instilled in them the value of equality, dignity of labor, and the importance of contributing to the community.

The wife of the guru symbolized compassion and care within the Gurukul, often acting as a motherly figure to the students. Through her actions, she taught lessons in humility, selflessness, and respect, underscoring the idea that true education transcends academics and encompasses the values that bind a community together.

This tradition reminds us that education is not merely about acquiring knowledge but about cultivating virtues that lead to harmony and equality in society.

III. **The Wife Of A Brāhmaṇa- Brāhmaṇi: - A Reflection Of Maya**

In the rich traditions of Hindu philosophy and culture, a brāhmaṇa is someone who dedicates their life to spiritual pursuits, scholarly study of the Vedas (sacred texts), and the performance of religious duties, including conducting rituals and offering sacrifices. The wife of a brāhmaṇa, known as the *brāhmaṇi* holds an equally revered place in this sacred framework. Her role, deeply rooted in devotion and service, is regarded as parallel to that of a mother, a nurturer, guide, and protector of spiritual values.

To understand the significance of the brāhmaṇi, it's helpful to draw a parallel to the wife of a guru, the spiritual teacher. While a guru serves as a formal mentor to students, offering education and guidance, a brāhmaṇa may not always function as a teacher in the same sense. Instead, brāhmanas often devote themselves to various spiritual practices, such as performing sacrifices, studying and preserving ancient wisdom, and guiding others in religious ceremonies. Despite these differences, the reverence for a brāhmaṇi remains steadfast, as her role is integral to sustaining the spiritual essence of her household and community.

The brāhmaṇi is far more than a passive observer. She is an active participant in the spiritual and cultural life of her family and society. Through her support, wisdom, and devotion, she helps preserve sacred traditions and ensures that the knowledge and values enshrined in the Vedas are passed on to future generations. Just as a mother nurtures her child's body and spirit, the brāhmaṇi nurtures the spiritual and moral foundation of her family and community.

The inclusion of Maya, a concept central to Hindu philosophy, adds a deeper dimension to the role of the brāhmaṇi. Maya is often described as the illusion of the material world, a force that can obscure the ultimate spiritual reality. The brāhmaṇi's life reflects a delicate balance: while engaged in worldly duties, she remains anchored in spiritual truth. Her humility, service, and ability to see beyond the illusions of material existence make her a living embodiment of the interplay between the temporal and the eternal.

IV. **The Wife Of The King: Rāja-Patnikā – Respect For The Position**

The wife of the king, known as the *rāja-patnikā*, holds a position of immense honor and reverence. Her role is not merely symbolic but deeply entrenched in the responsibility and influence she wields as the partner to the sovereign. This respect for the position extends beyond her individual identity, acknowledging her as a figure of maternal care and guidance for the people, akin to a mother's role in nurturing and protecting her children.

To make this relatable to today's world, consider the concept of the First Lady. In the United States, the First Lady holds an honorary title that signifies respect and recognition, not just for the person but for her association with the President, who is entrusted with leading the nation. Even those who may disagree with the President's policies understand the importance of protecting and respecting the office, as it represents the unity and security of the country. Similarly, the rāja-patnikā is deeply tied to the power and responsibility of the monarchy, and her position commands respect as part of the larger institution of leadership.

The rāja-patnikā is often seen as a unifying figure, bridging the monarchy and its subjects. Her association with power is not solely about authority; it reflects the care, compassion, and moral guidance expected from a maternal figure. In this way, she is regarded as a mother to the people, a nurturer of their welfare and a protector of their interests.

The inclusion of 'Respect for the Position' in this context underscores the importance of honoring the responsibilities and symbolic weight carried by individuals in such roles. While the person occupying the position may change, the reverence for the role itself remains constant, rooted in the values of dignity, service, and leadership.

Recognizing the rāja-patnikā's position reminds us the broader societal values that transcend individual identities. It is not just the person but the principles they represent, care, unity, and guidance, that command respect. The rāja-patnikā teaches us that true leadership is not only about wielding power but about embodying the ideals that bind a community together, reflecting the timeless essence of respect for the position.

V. **The Cow- Dhenuḥ – Nurture The Resources**

The cow, or *dhenuḥ*, holds a revered position in many cultures, particularly in Hinduism, as a symbol of fertility, wealth, and life. Often referred to as the 'mother-ancestor,' the cow was the first creature domesticated by humans. This sacred animal embodies the principle of nurturing resources, providing essential goods for human sustenance and well-being.

The Vedas emphasize the importance of the cow by detailing the four key products it offers, each vital to human life and the ecosystem:

a. **Milk**:

Cow's milk is a complete nutritional source, rich in fats, carbohydrates, minerals, and Vitamin B, all of which are crucial for human growth and health. According to Ayurveda, cow's milk has unique properties, such as the ability to increase radiation resistance and regenerate brain cells, underscoring its vital role in nurturing both physical and mental well-being.

b. **Ghee (Clarified Butter)**:

Considered the best type of ghee in Ayurveda, clarified butter from cow's milk is highly valued for its medicinal properties. It is believed to aid in curing numerous illnesses, supporting digestion, and improving overall vitality, making it an indispensable resource for holistic health.

c. **Gomutra (Cow Urine)**:

Cow urine, known for its remarkable medicinal properties, is utilized in treating various diseases. It possesses anti-cancer, anti-bacterial, anti-fungal, and antioxidant properties. Additionally, its immune-modulating capabilities make it particularly beneficial for combating immune deficiency disorders.

d. **Gomaya (Cow Dung)**:

Cow dung is an invaluable resource for agriculture, serving as an organic and nutrient-rich fertilizer that supports the growth of all plant varieties, from grains to fruits and vegetables. Beyond promoting sustainable farming, cow dung rejuvenates soil health, eliminating the need for chemical fertilizers and ensuring ecological balance.

The concept of 'Nurture the Resources' aligns seamlessly with the cow's role in human life. The cow exemplifies a perfect cycle of sustainability, where every by-product is not only utilized but cherished for its contributions to health, agriculture, and the environment. This principle teaches us the importance of valuing and nurturing the natural resources that sustain us, rather than exploiting them recklessly.

The cow serves as a living testament to the philosophy of sustainability and resource stewardship, urging us to embrace a lifestyle that nurtures and protects the planet.

VI. **The Nurse – A Mother's Care In Action**

In the context of motherhood, the role of a nurse can be seen as an extension of maternal care and compassion. While society has progressed to recognize that nursing is a profession open to all genders, the essence of the role is deeply rooted in qualities traditionally associated with mothers, unconditional care, patience, and selflessness.

The nurse provides essential, life-sustaining assistance, often behind the scenes and without acknowledgment. Much like a mother's role, the contributions of a nurse are crucial yet frequently taken for granted. They serve with unwavering dedication, even when the patients in their care are irritable, uncooperative, or ungrateful, paralleling a mother's ability to nurture her children through tantrums, challenges, and struggles.

A mother, like a nurse, often works tirelessly, putting the needs of others before her own, ensuring the well-being of those in her care. The emotional resilience and strength required in nursing mirror the sacrifices and perseverance that define motherhood.

Whether in the home or the hospital, the spirit of nurturing and healing reflects the essence of motherhood– an enduring commitment to support and uplift others, even in the face of adversity.

VII. **The Earth – The Embodiment Of Tolerance**

In many cultures and traditions, including the Vedic tradition, the Earth is revered as a mother, often referred to as *Bhumi Devi*, the goddess who presides over the material world. This idea reflects a universal truth– the Earth sustains all life, providing nourishment, shelter, and resources, much like a mother does for her child.

The Earth embodies tolerance in its truest sense. Despite enduring relentless exploitation, pollution, and disregard, she continues to sustain life, offering an abundance of grains, fruits, and other resources essential for survival. Just as a mother endures the challenges of raising her children, often without complaint, the Earth tolerates humanity's missteps and provides for us unconditionally.

These parallels highlight her role as a life-giver. The Earth produces seeds and sustains the cycles of nature, ensuring the continuity of life across generations. She demands little in return, embodying selflessness and resilience, key characteristics of motherhood.

Recognizing the Earth as a mother reminds us of the reverence she deserves. It calls for gratitude and a sense of responsibility to protect and nurture her, just as she has done for us. The embodiment of tolerance, the Earth, stands as a powerful symbol of motherhood, patience, and the unyielding commitment to life.

Through my journey, I will take you into the seven roles of a mother in today's world: Unconditional Love, Equality, Reflection of Maya, Respect, Nurture the Resources, The Nurse, and The Embodiment of Tolerance, sharing the wisdom and lessons I've gained along the way.

Chapter I
Unconditional Love

"You never know how much your parents loved you until you have a child to love."

– Jennifer Hudson

It's true what they say, you never truly understand the depth of your parents' love until you hold your own child in your arms. My mother once shared this wisdom with me, though at the time, I was too young to grasp its significance. Yet, in the circle of love that came with fatherhood, I found not only a profound understanding of my parents but also a renewed appreciation for the enduring power of a mother's wisdom.

Six days after my daughter's birth, a day of joyous celebration in our culture that symbolizes the child's official welcome into the family, I was struck by an unexpected wave of reflection. As I held my newborn, her tiny fingers curling around mine, I was reminded of a moment from my childhood, a moment that had once seemed insignificant but now carried profound meaning.

A few incidents stay with us forever, etched into memory–and for me, one of them goes back to fifth grade. In a burst of childish impulsiveness, I accused my mother of not loving me–a bold and thoughtless declaration. Calmly and with a knowing look in her eyes, she replied, "One day you'll be a parent."

Those words, spoken so casually at the time, were a mysterious whisper that lingered in the quiet corners of my mind.

For years, that phrase slumbered in my memory, buried beneath the restlessness of youth and the distractions of adulthood. It wasn't until 2009 that I found myself stepping into the role of a father that its true meaning blossomed. The veil of misunderstanding lifted, and I could finally see the depth of my mother's love, the selflessness, the quiet sacrifices, and the strength it took to guide and nurture me, even when I didn't recognize it.

That day, as I celebrated my daughter's life, I also celebrated a revelation, a profound moment of gratitude for my mother's wisdom, patience, and unconditional love. In the circle of life and love, I had come full circle, carrying forward the lessons she had imparted, now with a deeper understanding etched into my heart.

Reflecting on motherhood as it was fifty years ago, I can't help but feel a deep sense of respect for the women who lived those roles–often guided by the customs and expectations of their communities. To me, motherhood back then wasn't just about raising a child–it was about holding together the very fabric of the family, usually without recognition, and often in silence.

In many cultures, it was more than a role; it was a sacred duty, woven into the traditions and values that shaped daily life. For example, studies show that in the mid-20th century, especially in collectivist societies such as those in South Asia, Africa, and Latin America, extended family structures meant that motherhood carried communal responsibilities, with mothers often acting as pillars of social cohesion.

The way mothers showed love–unwavering, selfless, and often sacrificial–was deeply influenced by the world around them. Research into maternal behavior across cultures reveals that expressions of love can vary widely, from physical nurturing to acts of service and sacrifice, shaped largely by cultural norms. Their expression of care came through responsibility, resilience, and devotion, molded by the norms of their society. For instance, anthropologists have noted that in many traditional societies, the mother's role involved balancing the demands of household labor, child-rearing, and maintaining family honor—all without much public acknowledgment.

Of course, this is just my perspective, shaped by the stories I've heard, the lives I've witnessed, and the cultural lens I carry. It may differ from others' experiences, depending on where they come from or how they were raised. But in my heart, I believe that across time and culture, the quiet strength of mothers has always spoken the loudest.

For instance, in societies where family lineage and social status were highly valued, mothers demonstrated their love by meticulously preparing their sons for specific trades or professions and their daughters for their future roles as brides and mothers. This cultural emphasis on familial continuity and societal contribution defined the way affection and care were expressed.

Mothers were seen as the custodians of culture, passing down traditions, rituals, and values through their nurturing and teaching. In some traditions, this meant weaving folk tales and moral lessons into daily life, while in others, it involved adhering to strict gender roles that aligned with societal expectations.

The cultural lens not only shaped motherhood but also amplified its significance, tying it to the survival and prosperity of both family and community.

The survival and well-being of children in subsistence-based communities were deeply intertwined with the nature of maternal love, especially in societies where resources were scarce. A mother's love extended beyond meeting her children's physical needs; it encompassed teaching essential life skills such as food production, fostering self-reliance, and instilling resilience to navigate life's challenges.

Similarly, in traditional civilizations steeped in cultural heritage, mothers expressed their love by acting as custodians of ancestral wisdom. Through the transmission of language, rituals, and cultural practices, they ensured that the legacy of their forebears endured. This act of cultural preservation not only fortified a child's sense of identity but also symbolized the enduring link between maternal devotion and the survival of a community's cultural identity.

These varied expressions of maternal love from a few decades ago reveal the profound relationship between cultural norms and the ways love was demonstrated. They highlight how unconditional love was shaped by the social and cultural fabric of the time, varying significantly across different societal contexts.

Raising a child in a collectivist, subsistence-based society was not just about ensuring survival but also about nurturing the continuation of cultural traditions, preserving a legacy for generations to come.

Cultures had/have different expectations for mothers regarding discipline, independence, and sacrifice. The concept of a mother's love and its expression vary across cultures, even though the core idea of strong emotional attachment is common.

Time flows like a river, never pausing, always moving forward, carrying with it the stories of those who came before. In the same way, the essence of motherhood flows through generations, shaping the present while nurturing the future. Just as a river carries nutrients to the soil, sustaining life along its banks, a mother transfers values, wisdom, and unconditional love, ensuring the continuity of life's lessons and the persistence of cultural identity.

Mothers much like rivers, are anchors of change and constants of stability. They adapt to the demands of time, guiding, protecting, and flowing tirelessly to ensure the next generation finds its way. In every bend of life's journey, their nurturing influence acts as a gentle current, pushing us toward resilience, growth, and self-discovery.

As one generation passes its torch to the next, mothers serve as both the carriers and the creators of light, connecting the past to the future in an unbroken chain of care and purpose. In their embrace, the tide of shifting time finds a sanctuary, a timeless reminder that love and nurture are forces as enduring as the river's flow.

The guidance and upbringing provided by my mother went beyond typical gender stereotypes to make me a better parent, not just a better father. She cultivated a viewpoint that emphasized equality and shared responsibility, instilling in me the values and abilities necessary for accepting the responsibilities of parenthood. Her innovative strategy for shattering the myth of motherhood was much ahead of its time, establishing the groundwork for a more accepting and progressive conception of what it means to be a parent.

I don't recall my mom ever saying, "I love you." Yet, her love was evident in every action she took, especially through her passion for cooking. Preparing meals wasn't just a chore for her; it was her way of nurturing us and expressing her devotion to me and my siblings. She poured her heart into crafting balanced, homemade breakfasts like fresh parathas with some green vegetables, poha, and other classic North Indian dishes. Store bought breakfast options even the breads were almost unheard of in our home. For example, a small pack of cookies, commonly known as biscuits in India, would last us nearly two weeks, cherished as an occasional treat. Today, it's not uncommon for such a pack to be consumed in one sitting. This simple yet significant difference highlights the values my mother instilled in us- mindful consumption, appreciation for homemade nourishment, and the love woven into every meal she prepared.

Her passion for cooking extended to the school lunches she meticulously prepared for us every single day. Each lunchbox was thoughtfully packed with wholesome meals designed to keep us nourished and energized. Most often, it contained puris or parathas, homemade Indian bread, paired with stir-fried vegetables.

At the time, schools didn't have canteens, and every student was required to bring lunch from home. We were given just 30 minutes to finish eating and still squeeze in a quick play session. Those 30 minutes often felt rushed, a blur of eating and laughter with friends, but they also magnified the significance of what was packed in our lunchboxes.

I remember, though, feeling a pang of shame during my elementary and middle school years, embarrassed by my homemade lunch. It seemed to pale in comparison to the snacks my classmates brought, packaged and unhealthy but somehow 'cooler' in the eyes of a schoolkid. Perhaps it was my introverted nature or the silent pressure to fit in at the lunch table that made me wish for something different.

Looking back, I see my lunchbox for what it truly was, a treasure of love and care. Each bite was a reminder of her thoughtfulness and dedication.

Cooking wasn't just a duty for her; it was a source of joy, a way to nurture and provide, and an unspoken expression of her love. Through her food, she gave us so much more than sustenance; she gave us warmth, comfort, and a legacy of care that I hold close even today.

Perhaps this is why, as a father, I took it upon myself to prepare breakfast for my kids every morning, just as healthy and nourishing as possible. I wanted them to feel that same warmth, that same sense of being cared for, that I once felt when my mother packed my lunch. It's not just about feeding them; it's about offering them my love and care in the same way she did for me, through the simple, powerful act of food.

Her willingness to perform unpleasant tasks and run errands without being asked revealed her deep commitment–consistently placing our comfort and welfare above her own. Her unwavering support showed itself time and again, especially on nights when she stayed up late, sacrificing her own rest to help us finish a project or prepare for an exam, ensuring we had the best chance to succeed. These selfless and tender acts were quiet testaments of her boundless love–love we all too often, took for granted.

What is Love?

"If your love is there to help others, nobody can destroy it. But if your love is to get something from the other - sooner or later - it will be broken into pieces."

–Sri Sri Ravi Shankar, the spiritual leader and founder of the Art of Living Foundation.

The voyage of love begins even before the first breath is taken, and it is based on the protective and nurturing instincts of a mother. This first tie, created in the holy cocoon of pregnancy, lays the groundwork for a loving and devoted relationship that lasts a lifetime.

As life unfolds, love evolves and deepens, transcending mere transactions or exchanges. It is not a commodity to be bartered but rather a boundless reservoir of compassion, empathy, and understanding. Unlike fleeting transactions that seek reciprocity, genuine love flows unconditionally, enriching both the giver and the receiver. Through the lens of motherhood, this profound truth becomes even more evident. A mother's love is unconditional and transcends all concepts of give and take. It is an enduring, selfless energy that shapes the very fabric of existence while empowering, nurturing, and guarding against harm.

In exploring the essence of love, I come to realize that its essence lies not in transactions but in the pure, unadulterated expression of the heart, a timeless, boundless wellspring that sustains and uplifts us on life's journey.

My mother's wise words often echo in my mind, especially during moments of reflection. She taught me that when we look back on a situation, it's easy to pass judgment on whether it was right or wrong. However, in doing so, we often lose sight of the context of time.

One morning, during my usual call with my mom, our conversation unexpectedly turned to one of my aunts. I quickly interjected, expressing my dislike for her and my unwillingness to even discuss her. My reasoning was simple: I always felt overlooked by her, as if I didn't exist in her world.

My mom, unaware of the bitterness I harbored, was taken aback by my outburst. Her response, however, was both insightful and profound.

She gently probed further, trying to understand the root of my feelings, and eventually uncovered a naive incident from my childhood. I reminded her of a time when I wasn't allowed to play with my cousin. As a child, I had assumed the reason that my aunt didn't want her son to associate with me, likely because I wasn't good at studies. This assumption had cemented itself in my mind, feeding my resentment over the years. However, my mom explained that my cousin wasn't allowed to play because his mother had her own unrelated concerns, something completely different from what I had imagined.

We both laughed at the absurdity of my long-held belief. My mom then offered me a piece of wisdom that struck a chord.

She said, "This is all in your mind. Everyone else has long since moved on, except you. Don't seek forgiveness from others, rather, forgive yourself and let it go."

Her words reminded me of the power of self-reflection and the importance of releasing unnecessary burdens, especially those rooted in misunderstanding.

She said that while assigning blame for the behavior of others may seem easy, it often overlooks the intricate settings that shaped their decisions. People act in response to specific situations, encountering obstacles and challenges that influence their decision-making. It's essential to take a step back and evaluate the larger picture–the context in which those decisions were made. What was the person going through at that very moment? What obstacles or limitations were they up against? Comprehending these variables enables us to develop empathy for others and acquire a more profound comprehension of their behaviors.

Her words stayed with me long after our conversation ended, reminding me of the importance of looking beyond my own perspective. Time and again, Mom kept reminding me in her own subtle way that as we navigate life's reflections, remember to take a moment to understand before judging others. Dive deep into the complexities of human experiences with empathy and a keen eye for context. Through this lens, uncover invaluable insights about yourself and others, nurturing a path of wisdom and compassion. Embrace each discovery with an open heart and a curious mind, for therein lies the essence of true understanding.

"*Those who are free from anger and all attachment, who are balanced in pleasure and pain, and who are forgiving, constantly focused, contented, and self-controlled, are said to be established in intrinsic love.*" –(Bhagavad Gita 12.13)

"*For God so loved the world that he gave his one and only Son, that whoever believes in him shall not perish but have eternal life.*" - John 3:16 (NIV)

This verse emphasizes the depth and selfless nature of God's love, which is considered intrinsic and unconditional.

Even though my mom's metaphors appeared superficially simple or meaningless, they frequently had deep meaning and thought provoking insights.

My mother once reminded me of a profound question that was posed to Buddha: "What is the difference between saying 'I like you' and 'I love you'?" His answer was beautifully simple – "When you like a flower, you just pluck it. But when you love a flower, you water it daily!"

As I reflected on this analogy within the context of motherhood, I realized that the essence of a mother's love transcends mere affection; it embodies a continuous act of nurturing that begins long before a child is born. It starts when a woman first harbors thoughts of motherhood in the depths of her heart and soul. From that moment onward, love takes root and blossoms, evolving into a lifelong journey of care, sacrifice, and unwavering devotion.

A mother's nurturing love is characterized by innumerable moments of kindness, selflessness, and tenacity, which are what truly define the link between a mother and her child. With each tender gesture and comforting embrace, it is a love that shapes a child's own essence. It fosters not only their physical health but also their emotional, spiritual, and intellectual development.

In our heartfelt conversation about the essence of motherly love, I raised a counterpoint to the notion that everything originating from within is inherently good. I compared this subtle phenomenon to cancer, emphasizing that both have internal origins and have the potential to spread uncontrollably. My illustration was meant to illustrate the intricacy of internal workings and their capacity for both beneficial and detrimental results.

My mother, much to my astonishment, accepted my viewpoint. Anything in excess, she said, might cause imbalance and unfavorable effects, whether it be love or cellular proliferation. She made an affecting comparison between the unbridled spread of cancer cells and the unbridled blooming of love. Abnormal affection for a person or thing can become an obsession or a kind of madness, just as unchecked cancer spreads and upsets the body's equilibrium.

Our conversation emphasized the need for love to be balanced and moderated, pointing out that although love is a strong force for healing and connection, an unchecked excess of it can have negative effects. It reminded me that love needs boundaries, careful attention, and a thoughtful approach to grow without overwhelming the heart and soul, just like taking care of a fragile garden.

She shared with me a timeless truth- "Your children do not belong to you; they are born from life's deep yearning to realize and reflect itself..." These words, resonant with wisdom and humility, spoke volumes about the profound nature of parenthood and the interconnectedness of life's journey.

In that moment, I felt a surge of gratitude for her wisdom and guidance, realizing that her role as a mother transcended mere ownership or control but encompassed a deep-seated nurturing of life's essence. Her words echoed with a gentle reminder that while I came through her, my path and purpose were uniquely mine, intertwined with the universal longing for growth and self-discovery.

My Mother encouraged me to embrace my journey with sincerity and purpose, understanding that even though I walk with her, my presence is a monument to Life's unending need for itself. Her message was one of great release and responsibility.

"*Your children are not your children. They are the sons and daughters of Life's longing for itself...*" Kahlil Gibran, a Lebanese-American writer, poet, and philosopher.

I learned that a relationship with my mother is not just a biological process but a spiritual and emotional journey. It was an exploration of the heart's capacity for unconditional love, a theme that resonates with the essence of my mother's prophecy. The tapestry of love, woven between generations, revealed a path to understanding, forgiveness and appreciation.

In the corporate world, the principles of unconditional love translate into valuable business lessons that foster trust, loyalty, and enduring relationships.

- **Leadership Through Nurturing**: Growing up, I witnessed my mother's unwavering dedication to our well-being. This taught me that leadership isn't just about directing but nurturing. In business, I've learned that nurturing my team, understanding their strengths, offering support, and fostering their growth, is essential. Just as my mother's love helped me flourish, a leader's support can help employees reach their full potential.

- **Cultural Sensitivity And Adaptability**: The cultural nuances of maternal love taught me the importance of understanding and respecting differences. In a business context, being culturally sensitive and adaptable is crucial. Whether dealing with international clients or diverse teams, appreciating cultural differences can lead to more effective communication and stronger relationships.

- **Embracing A Long-term Vision**: Just as my mother prepared us for the future, I've learned to focus on long-term goals in business. This involves looking beyond immediate profits and considering sustainable growth, future market trends, and the long-term well-being of the company and its employees.

- **Empathy As A Cornerstone**: Reflecting on my mother's empathy has shown me its power in understanding others' perspectives and actions. In business, empathy helps in managing teams, resolving conflicts, and building a cohesive work environment.

Understanding the personal and professional challenges of employees fosters a supportive and collaborative workplace.

- **Striking A Balance**: The analogy of love and cancer taught me the importance of balance. In business, it's vital to balance ambition with ethics, innovation with tradition, and growth with sustainability. Just as unchecked growth can be harmful, businesses must ensure balanced and sustainable practices.

- **Empowering Others**: My mother empowered me to be independent and confident. In the business world, empowering employees, giving them autonomy, trust, and resources, leads to a more dynamic and innovative organization. Empowered employees are more likely to take the initiative, contribute ideas, and drive the company forward.

- **Emotional Intelligence**: The emotional intelligence my mother displayed in her actions has been a crucial lesson. In business, emotional intelligence, understanding and managing our own emotions and those of others, enhances leadership, team collaboration, and client relations. It's about being aware, empathetic, and constructive in interactions.

- **Preserving Core Values And Culture**: My mother's emphasis on cultural preservation resonates with the need to maintain core values in business. As companies grow and evolve, staying true to foundational values and culture ensures consistency, integrity, and a sense of identity, which attracts loyal customers and employees.
- **Fostering Resilience And Adaptability**: The resilience my mother instilled in me is a vital trait in business. Companies face constant challenges and changes, and fostering a culture of resilience and adaptability is key. Encouraging a mindset that views challenges as opportunities and adapts swiftly to changes can lead to sustained success.

Through these reflections, I realize that the lessons of unconditional love and the wisdom of my mother provide a profound framework for business leadership and management. By integrating these principles, we can create more humane, effective, and enduring business practices.

I wish I had taken the time to truly listen to my mom and cherish her wisdom while I had the chance.

Your Notes: Reflections on Your Own Experience with Parents.

Chapter II
Equality

"Equality is not in regarding different things similarly, equality is in regarding different things differently."

– Tom Robbins

During my first visit to my hometown in India after my mother passed away, I found myself reminiscing about her with our house manager. She had employed him not out of necessity, but as a way to help him earn his livelihood, providing him with a part-time job that offered additional support. We continue to employ him as a tribute to her legacy. As we talked, he shared something about my mother that illuminated a facet of her character I had not fully recognized before. He said, "Your mother had a remarkable quality, she treated everyone according to what they deserved."

This observation struck me profoundly. It was a reminder of how she treated every person she encountered with a deep sense of respect and fairness, tailoring her actions to honor their individual worth and contributions. Her approach was not about equal treatment in a generic sense, but rather about honoring each person's unique value and role in her life and the community.

At our home, a helper who was the son of our old-time cook from my grandmother's era would visit occasionally, either to check in or seek help. I used to call him *Chacha*, the Hindi word for Uncle. I enjoyed playing with him while growing up. My mom would always offer him some snacks or a meal, depending on the time of his visit. However, he never ate with us at the same table, nor did he sit on the same couch.

I vividly remember a time during my elementary school years when I asked my mom why Chacha couldn't sit with us. Mom was very fond of knitting, and she was working on a new scarf at that moment. She put down her knitting, her heart heavy with the realization that the time had come to explain some of life's harsh truths to her son. She pulled me closer, her hand gently resting on my shoulder.

She explained that in India, traditional social structures—particularly the caste system—had long influenced the way people interacted with each other. Originating thousands of years ago, the caste system divided society into hierarchical groups, with rigid expectations about occupation, status, and purity. Those considered to be from 'lower castes' or engaged in certain types of labor—such as cooking, cleaning, or other service work—were often socially excluded, even if they were deeply woven into the life of a household.

Sitting together, eating from the same utensils, or sharing a table were seen as breaches of social boundaries, rooted in notions of ritual purity and inherited inequality.

In many families, this extended beyond caste to class as well. Even if someone wasn't from a different caste, their occupation and perceived status often defined their social distance. These customs, though widely accepted for generations, were not rooted in kindness or fairness—they were products of a deeply stratified society that limited dignity based on birth.

But my mother also shared that the world was changing. Education, urbanization, constitutional reforms, and social justice movements had begun to shift the narrative. The Indian Constitution, adopted in 1950, outlawed untouchability and guaranteed equality. Activists and reformers across decades challenged these divisions. And in cities like ours, new generations were starting to question and unlearn these inherited prejudices. More people were now choosing inclusion over exclusion–eating together, working together, and forming friendships that transcended caste and class.

That moment stayed with me. It opened my eyes not only to the inequalities of the past but also to the power of reflection and change. Chacha wasn't just our helper–he was part of our story. And while we can't rewrite the past, we can certainly shape the future.

"Our world is like this scarf I'm knitting," she began, her hands gently picking up a skein of yarn. "Each thread represents a person, unique in its own color, texture, and strength. Some threads are bold and bright, while others are soft and subtle. Each one is different, and that's what makes them special. Yet, when woven together, they create something far more beautiful and resilient than any single strand could on its own. No thread is more important than another; they all contribute to the tapestry. It's the harmony of these differences, the way they blend and support one another, that forms the strength and beauty of the scarf. Just like in our world, every person matters, and every contribution is valuable."

I listened intently, my young mind working to process her words. I'm sure I didn't fully understand the deeper meaning of our conversation at that time, but some moments have a way of embedding themselves in our memories, and this was one of those moments for me. My early struggles with reading and writing often left me more time to think, allowing these memories to settle deeply in my mind.

Years later, during my daily phone calls with my mom–a cherished ritual during my morning commute to work, which coincided with her evening in India–I often found myself revisiting those childhood memories, recalling her words and the lessons they carried.

To my surprise, she remembered each conversation just as clearly as I did. I would often ask, “How do you remember all of this?” She would always reply with the same two phrases– “I am your mother,” and “Just as you remember, I remember too.”

“In our society,” Mom continued, over our phone conversation that felt like we resumed the 25+ year old conversation, “some people believe that certain threads belong at the center and others on the edges, just because of their background or caste. But this is not true. Every person deserves respect and kindness, no matter who they are or where they come from.”

"Mom, I was thinking about Chacha today," I said over the phone, my voice filled with curiosity. "Why did he always have to sit separately back then?" Though I already understood the reasons, for me, our conversation felt like a time machine, transporting us back to those moments.

Mom sighed softly at the other end; her voice warm but tinged with a hint of sadness.

"Beta," a Hindi word for son, at times my mom used to say beta to me in conversation, "sometimes people hold onto old ways because they're afraid of change. Even today, many cling to those outdated beliefs. But it's our responsibility, as the next generation, to create a new pattern, one where everyone is treated as equal and valued."

I could almost picture her sitting with her knitting needles, her hands working methodically as she spoke in the past. "You know, like the scarf I used to knit. Each thread is unique in its own way, but together, they create something beautiful and strong. You can make a difference by treating everyone with kindness and respect. When you stand up for people like Chacha, you're helping to weave a stronger, more beautiful fabric."

I nodded, even though she couldn't see me. Her words resonated deeply, stirring a sense of determination within me. “You’re right, Mom. It’s up to us to make those changes, isn’t it?”

“Exactly,” she replied softly, her voice filled with warmth and encouragement. “Through the small actions you take and the understanding you cultivate, there’s hope for a future where equality and compassion lead the way. Every step count, beta.”

As we continued to talk, I realized that our conversation was more than just catching up; it was a powerful reminder of the values she had instilled in me and a call to action. Her words and lessons weren’t just memories, they were seeds planted for a better tomorrow.

As mentioned in the introduction, in Vedic times, the wife of the spiritual master, the ‘Guroḥ-patnī,’ was revered as a maternal figure. In today’s modern era, where the Gurukul system has almost disappeared, the role of a mother encompasses the nurturing and guiding qualities once embodied by the wife of the spiritual master. A mother has worn multiple hats in today’s world.

In the Vedic system of the Gurukul, the wife of the spiritual master or teacher, the ‘Gurupatni’, played an important and multifaceted role within the educational and spiritual community. Her responsibilities extended beyond the domestic sphere, significantly contributing to the overall functioning and nurturing environment of the Gurukul.

The Gurupatni often acted as a motherly figure to the students (shishyas) who lived and studied there, providing emotional support, guidance, and care, creating a homely atmosphere for those away from their families. While the primary instruction was given by the Guru, the Gurupatni might have also assisted in teaching, especially in areas related to domestic skills, moral values, and spiritual practices, helping inculcate discipline, respect, and humility. She was responsible for managing the daily household activities, including cooking, cleaning, and ensuring that the students' basic needs were met, allowing the Guru to focus on imparting knowledge without worrying about domestic concerns.

The Gurupatni participated in and supported the religious and spiritual practices conducted at the Gurukul, performing rituals, maintaining sacred spaces, and ensuring students adhered to their spiritual disciplines. Additionally, the Gurupatni sometimes acted as a mediator and counselor for the students, helping resolve conflicts and providing guidance on personal issues; her wisdom and experience being invaluable in nurturing the students' growth and development.

As the wife of the Guru, she was seen as a role model, exemplifying virtues such as devotion, service, and piety, setting an example for the students to emulate. In summary, the Guru Patni's role in the Vedic system of the Gurukul was integral to the holistic development of the students, providing a nurturing, supportive, and morally enriching environment that complemented the Guru's educational and spiritual teachings.

Similarly, my mother played a role in our home that mirrored the Gurupatni's responsibilities and influence. She was not just a caregiver but also a nurturer and guide. Just like the Gurupatni, my mother created a warm, homely atmosphere where everyone felt valued and respected. I remember how she took whosoever visited our home, which was almost daily. She always ensured everyone had food if not then at least a glass of water or tea 'Chai'. Her kindness and hospitality were evident in every small gesture.

Beyond her domestic responsibilities, my mother was deeply involved in my education and moral upbringing. She would often share stories that conveyed important life lessons, just like the Gurupatni who assisted in teaching values and spiritual practices to the students. Her words were imbued with wisdom, teaching me about respect, humility, and compassion.

Managing the household was another area where my mother excelled, like the Gurupatni's role in the Gurukul. She took care of all the daily activities, from cooking and cleaning to ensuring that the house ran smoothly. My mother also played a significant role in supporting our family's spiritual and religious practices. She maintained our sacred spaces with reverence, participated in rituals, and ensured that I adhered to our spiritual disciplines. Her devotion was a constant reminder of the importance of faith and spirituality in our lives.

Above all, my mother was a role model. Her conduct, filled with virtues such as devotion, service, piety, and the tacit knowledge set an example for me to follow. She demonstrated through her actions and wisdom how to live a life of integrity and compassion.

In reflecting on my mother's role, I realize how much she mirrored the Gurupatni's role in the Gurukul. She provided a nurturing, supportive, and morally enriching environment that complemented my educational journey. Her efforts laid the foundation for a future where equality and compassion reigned, just as the Gurupatni did for the students in the ancient Vedic system.

My mother's role as a mediator and counselor extended far beyond our immediate family. She was the go-to person for resolving conflicts and providing heartfelt guidance not only within our family but also among our extended relatives and even my father's circle of friends. Her wisdom, grounded in experience and empathy, made her a trusted confidante for those around her.

It became a running joke in our household that she was the family's unpaid therapist and counselor. We would tease her about being everyone's personal advisor without ever raising an invoice. But in truth, her ability to mediate delicate situations and offer advice with such patience and clarity was nothing short of remarkable. Whether it was bridging differences between siblings, helping relatives through their marital challenges, or offering a listening ear to a friend's grievances, she approached every situation with the same sincerity and dedication.

Watching her take on this unofficial role taught me the importance of empathy, active listening, and finding common ground, skills that would later become invaluable in my own life. Through her actions, she demonstrated that sometimes the greatest impact is made not through grand gestures but through quiet, consistent acts of understanding and care.

During a call with my mom, she shared how she was mediating a property dispute between two brothers. She admitted that while she was doing her best to resolve the situation, the effort took a toll on her.

From time to time, she would remind me about the importance of maintaining balance in life. In her characteristically sarcastic tone, she'd say, "Don't be selfish, but don't be overcommitted either. It's a fine line you'll have to learn to walk."

Naturally, I asked her the obvious question, "How do you find that balance?"

Her response was simple yet profound. "There's no secret recipe. Everyone's journey is unique, and each person has to figure it out for themselves."

Her words have stayed with me, a reminder that life's balance isn't something handed to you, it's something you discover and refine as you grow.

In the spring of 2017, my parents were visiting the US to attend my MBA graduation. It was an ordinary call, but a few days before their departure, my mother mentioned that her layover would be in Paris. It wasn't her first time passing through Paris, so she was well-versed in navigating the airport and handling the flight changes. My father was traveling with her, but he suffered from travel anxiety and was entirely dependent on her.

I asked, "Mom, all set for the travel?"

Her answer was a confident "Yes."

I teased her a bit, "You're an experienced traveler now! You've navigated airports in the Netherlands, Frankfurt, and Paris. You've got this."

Despite not knowing French, Dutch, or German, my mother always managed to communicate without issues.

Our conversation then drifted to memories from my elementary school days. I remembered how, during parent-teacher meetings, my father always accompanied my mother, simply because she wasn't fluent in English. I had once asked her, "Mom, why can't you speak English better?" Her answer has echoed in my mind ever since– "How does it matter?"

Returning to our conversation in 2017, I apologized.

"I'm sorry for saying that to you when I was younger."

There was a brief pause, and then she replied, "It's okay." After a moment of silence, she added, "For you and many others, English is more than just a language–it's a skillset. I don't have that, but I'm proud that you all do. That's all that matters. No one in this world has every skillset."

Her words stayed with me, reminding me of the importance of perspective and the value of what we often take for granted.

I was reflecting on why Mom referred to English as a skill. Applying my Six Sigma problem-solving mindset, I asked myself 'why' five times and arrived at an interesting realization.

When I write software programs, I first read and understand the requirements and the problems, then process my thoughts before converting them into a programming language. In the past, when I worked with SAP ABAP, I followed its syntax to structure my code. Similarly, in daily life, I sometimes think in Hindi, while other times, I interpret symbols or signs and then translate those signals into English.

With this analogy in mind, isn't English more than just a language for most people whose first language isn't English? Doesn't it often function as a skill, one that opens doors, creates opportunities, and sometimes even defines competence in ways beyond mere communication?

It was late spring of 2017, during the final days of my cohort MBA program. Those who have gone through such an intensive program would know that as it nears completion, a shift occurs, suddenly there's an unfamiliar abundance of free time. The once relentless cycle of assignments, readings, and deadlines vanishes, leaving behind a void where the constant demand for efficiency once thrived.

Balancing work, studies, and family had required mastering the art of creating extra hours in a day, and when it all ended, returning to my pre-MBA routine didn't seem natural. Instead, I found myself in a state of transition, my mind became more reflective than occupied.

That evening, as I was heading to bed, a thought struck me– "Why does the Lean Six Sigma problem-solving method emphasize," asking 'Why?' exactly five times. Why not three? Why not seven?

As with most questions in the modern world, I turned to Google, hoping for a concrete answer. I already knew that Lean and Six Sigma had strong roots in Japanese manufacturing, but I couldn't find a definitive reason behind the choice of five. However, one key takeaway stood out, by the time one reaches the fifth 'Why,' the process naturally forces deeper thinking while avoiding analysis paralysis.

The number five lingered in my thoughts that night. The next day, during my regular call with my mother, I abruptly asked, "Mom, does the number five hold any significance in Buddhism?" Without hesitation, she answered, "Yes."

Her response made perfect sense. Being from Bodh Gaya, the birthplace of Buddhism, I was aware of Japan's deep Buddhist influence.

I asked her to elaborate, and she explained that Buddhism, much like Hinduism, recognizes five fundamental elements: Earth, Water, Fire, Wind, and Space. Intrigued, we continued discussing Japan's cultural connection to this number.

Traditional Buddhist pagodas in Japan often have five tiers, each representing one of these elements. Even Japanese cuisine follows a principle of balance based on five flavors: Sweet, Sour, Salty, Bitter, and Umami.

Reflecting on this, I began to wonder, "Could it be that the Japanese professionals who developed the '5 Whys' method were subconsciously influenced by this deep-rooted cultural association with the number five?"

Perhaps, without explicitly realizing it, they had drawn upon an ancient philosophy that emphasized balance, structure, and depth of understanding. Maybe, just maybe, the power of 'five' in problem-solving wasn't a random choice but rather an unspoken acknowledgment of a principle woven into the very fabric of their culture.

One evening over dinner, my teenage daughter looked up from her plate and asked, "Dad, who was your favorite teacher?"

The question caught me off guard, and I paused, my fork hovering in mid-air as I thought about it. Memories of my school days flashed before my eyes, various teachers, each with their own unique style and influence. But as I sifted through the faces and lessons, one figure stood out more prominently than the rest.

I put my fork down and looked at my daughter. "My favorite teacher was my mother," I said, a smile spreading across my face.

She looked surprised, expecting perhaps the name of a school teacher.

I continued, "You see, my mother wasn't just a caregiver; she was my guide, my mentor, and my moral compass. Just like a teacher in a Gurukul, she taught me life's most valuable lessons, kindness, respect, humility, and the importance of treating everyone equally. She created a nurturing environment that allowed me to grow and learn in ways that went beyond textbooks."

My daughter listened intently as I shared stories of how my mother, much like the Gurupatni in the Vedic tradition, played a multifaceted role in our household. "She not only managed our home with meticulous care but also supported my educational and spiritual development. Her wisdom and guidance were instrumental in shaping the person I am today."

"As I think back," I concluded, "I realize that the lessons she imparted were far more profound and lasting than anything I learned in a classroom. She was the embodiment of patience, love, and unwavering support, a true teacher in every sense of the word."

My daughter smiled, perhaps seeing her grandmother in a new light, and we continued our dinner with a deeper understanding and appreciation of the lessons passed down through generations.

I remember it as if it happened yesterday, the year was 1989, the year my cousin was born. In our hometown, Gaya, a small city in India, it was customary for transgender families, often referred to as Hijras, to visit homes where a new child had been born to ask for money or gifts. This tradition was explained to me as part of the celebration of new life.

So, when my cousin was born, the Hijras visited, asking for their gratuity. They started with a high demand, as was customary, and my mother and uncle, my cousin's father, engaged in negotiation. I don't recall the exact amount or the gift they finally agreed upon, but what stands out vividly in my memory is that this was my first interaction with a transgender person, which sparked a multitude of questions in my young mind.

Later that evening, my mother noticed my contemplative mood and asked if I wanted to discuss anything. Nervously, I asked, "What does 'Hijra' mean?" Hijra is the Hindi word for transgender.

My mother's response was simple yet profound. She told me, "They are human, just like us, but God created them slightly different."

She reminded me of what I had learned from Sanskrit literature, explaining that in Sanskrit, there are three genders– 'Female', 'Male', and 'Neuter'.

In Sanskrit gender are often not aligns with biological sex, rather in Sanskrit, gender is a grammatical category assigned to nouns and adjectives, and it doesn't always correspond to the natural gender of the object it refers to.

She used this as a teaching moment, emphasizing that all humans are equal, regardless of their origin or identification.

Her words left a lasting impression on me. My mother's wisdom transcended the conventional norms of our society. She taught me that every individual, regardless of their gender identity, deserves respect and dignity. This lesson in equality was not just about understanding the existence of different genders but about recognizing the inherent worth of every person.

She continued, explaining that Hijras have a long and complex history in Indian culture, often occupying unique social and religious roles. They were not just defined by their gender identity but were also carriers of blessings and curses, performers, and spiritual figures. My mother highlighted the importance of respecting their place in society, despite the prejudices and misunderstandings that often surrounded them.

As I listened to her, I was struck by her empathy and understanding. She made it clear that discrimination and prejudice were born out of ignorance and fear. By treating everyone with kindness and respect, we could overcome these barriers and build a more inclusive society. Her lesson was a call to action for me to look beyond societal labels and see the humanity in everyone.

Reflecting on this memory, I realize how pivotal that conversation was in shaping my perspective. It was through my mother's gentle guidance and profound teachings that I learned to appreciate the rich tapestry of human identity and to advocate for a world where everyone is valued equally. Her lessons on equality went beyond just accepting differences; they were about celebrating them and recognizing the strength they bring to our collective human experience.

My mother's teachings were rooted in compassion and an unwavering belief in the fundamental equality of all people. She taught me to stand up against injustice and to always extend a hand of friendship and understanding to those who were marginalized. Her influence has been a guiding light in my life, shaping not only my personal values but also my approach to the world around me.

This early lesson in equality has stayed with me throughout my life, reminding me that the fight for dignity and respect for all is ongoing. It taught me the importance of listening, understanding, and advocating for those who may not have a voice. My mother's wisdom and compassion have inspired me to strive for a more inclusive and just society, one where every individual is celebrated for who they are.

Another profound lesson on equality that my mother imparted to me was one that initially made me feel uncomfortable and shy: buying sanitary napkins. My mother was responsible for the household groceries and other regular shopping. Either my sister or I would accompany her to the downtown market on a cycle rickshaw, a human-powered vehicle with pedals.

During these trips, amidst the vegetables, grains, and other essentials, sanitary napkins were always on her list. One day, curious and a bit embarrassed, I asked her about them. She explained that menstruation is a natural phenomenon that occurs in all females. It was a straightforward, matter-of-fact explanation, devoid of any awkwardness.

What struck me most wasn't just the information itself, but the deeper lesson she conveyed. My mother emphasized that menstruation is a regular, natural process and should be treated as such, without stigma or shame. She wanted me to understand that it was not something to be hidden or embarrassed about, but a normal part of life.

She made it clear that acknowledging and accepting menstruation without prejudice was part of treating everyone equally. It wasn't just about understanding a biological fact; it was about breaking down the societal taboos and misconceptions that often surround it. My mother believed that true equality meant addressing these issues openly and without bias, recognizing that these experiences are fundamental to the human condition and should not be seen as defining one's worth or capability.

Her approach to teaching me about menstruation was a small but significant part of her broader lesson on equality. She taught me that respecting others means understanding and accepting their experiences, even those that are different from my own. By normalizing conversations about menstruation, she was also challenging gender biases that often dictate what is considered appropriate to discuss or acknowledge.

Through these lessons, my mother instilled in me a sense of respect and empathy toward women and their experiences. She taught me to see beyond societal norms and prejudices, to understand that true equality involves recognizing and respecting the natural processes and challenges that everyone faces, regardless of gender.

Her wisdom extended beyond mere tolerance; it was about genuine acceptance and understanding. She wanted me to grow up seeing women as equals in every respect, deserving of the same dignity and consideration.

This lesson on sanitary napkins was not just about a product; it was about changing perceptions and fostering a culture of respect and equality.

Reflecting on these experiences, I realize how ahead of her time my mother was. She used everyday moments to teach profound lessons, breaking down complex societal issues into simple, understandable truths. Her teachings have stayed with me, guiding my actions and beliefs, and reinforcing the idea that equality is about more than just acknowledging differences, it's about embracing and respecting them.

Looking back, I wish I had spent more time with my mother and taken her words and their deeper meanings more seriously. I truly believe that if I had internalized her lessons, I would have been a better person today. Reflecting on our time together, I realize that she was trying to teach me the importance of empathy and the true essence of equality and equity.

One of the key lessons my mother imparted was the distinction between equality and equity. She often emphasized that while equality means treating everyone the same, equity involves recognizing that people come from different backgrounds and face different challenges and thus may need to be treated accordingly to achieve fairness.

Equality: Treating everyone the same, regardless of circumstances. My mother demonstrated this in her everyday interactions. Whether it was domestic help, the shopkeepers, or strangers, she treated everyone with the same level of respect and kindness. She wanted me to understand that every person deserves to be treated with dignity, irrespective of their social status or identity.

Equity: Recognizing that people come from different backgrounds, they might have different challenges and she treated them accordingly. My mother was also a strong advocate for equity. She would often go out of her way to help those in need, understanding that some people required extra support to overcome their difficulties. For example, she would offer additional assistance to children struggling in school, ensuring they had the resources and encouragement they needed to succeed. This was not just about fairness but about providing everyone with the opportunity to thrive.

By encouraging empathy, my mother taught me to see the world through others' eyes, to understand their struggles, and to respond with compassion. She believed that empathy was the foundation of true equality and equity. Her actions taught me that to build a just and inclusive society, we must be willing to recognize and address the unique challenges faced by individuals and offer support where it's needed most.

In reflecting on these lessons, I realize that my mother's teachings were not just about understanding societal concepts but about embodying them in everyday life. She showed me that empathy is not just a feeling but an action. It requires us to go beyond our own experiences, to listen, to learn, and to act in ways that uplift others.

One of the fundamental lessons I have learned, which we will delve into more deeply in the subsequent chapters, is the importance of balancing equality and equity with a sense of responsibility. It's increasingly apparent that discussions about equality and equity can sometimes be used as excuses to evade essential duties and responsibilities. For instance, in contemporary conversations, there is often a reluctance to engage in traditional roles such as cooking meals or raising children, which are seen by some as outdated or gender-specific responsibilities. However, the pursuit of equality and equity should not serve as a pretext for shirking these responsibilities.

True equality entails treating each person with the same level of respect and dignity, yet it does not mean that everyone's roles and responsibilities must be identical. Rather, it means valuing each role and contribution fairly.

This distinction is crucial because as society evolves and traditional roles are redefined, it's essential that we do not lose sight of the inherent value and necessity of these roles. Whether it's preparing a meal, caring for a child, or fulfilling other significant duties, these responsibilities should be embraced with purpose and dedication, not avoided.

Living in the U.S. with my wife and raising two kids born here, without the support of extended family, often left me feeling utterly exhausted. Managing household chores, cooking meals, and keeping up with the relentless demands of my job was no small feat. It wasn't just the work culture that pushed me to my limits; it was my own relentless drive to go above and beyond, to always do more than what was required.

In moments of sheer frustration and fatigue, I would call my mom and vent, "I wish you hadn't taught me how to do house chores and cooking. If I didn't know how to do all this, I wouldn't be pushing myself so hard."

Mom, always quick with a sharp response, would laugh and say, "So now it's my fault? Oh, come on, grow up!" But then her tone would shift, and she'd launch into one of her impassioned lectures, the kind that made you stop and think. "I raised my children as people, not as a boy or a girl," she'd say with conviction, her words striking like lightning.

Now, as I reflect on those words, especially with her no longer here to share them, I realize just how powerful and ahead of her time she was. She didn't see gender as a set of rigid roles or expectations.

To her, gender was just a concept, a role, perhaps assigned by God or some higher power for those who don't believe in God. But she never let it define us. She taught us to see beyond the labels, to see each other first and foremost as human beings.

Growing up, I never realized the depth of this lesson. But now, in raising my own kids, I see the world through her eyes. She wanted us to understand that true equality doesn't come from pretending gender doesn't exist but from recognizing and valuing each person for who they are, beyond the labels of 'male,' 'female,' or anything else.

I remember one conversation vividly. I was overwhelmed, trying to balance work, parenting, and everything else life was throwing at me.

"Why did you make me learn all these things?" I complained, half-joking, half-serious.

"Because I wanted you to be capable and independent," she shouted back, without missing a beat. "I wanted you to know that you can do anything, not just because of your gender but because of who you are."

Her words were a wake-up call. She never saw chores or cooking as 'women's work' or 'men's work.' To her, they were just life skills, things everyone should know, regardless of who they were. It was a radical idea, one that broke down traditional gender roles and expectations.

And now, as I look back on all those lessons, I see the true brilliance of her teaching. She was building a foundation for equality, one where every person is valued for their humanity, not their gender. She believed in a world where the first thing we notice about each other is our shared humanity, not the labels that society assigns us.

I often wish for a world where we could all adopt her perspective, a world where we see each other as people first, beyond gender, beyond roles, and beyond expectations.

Her teachings weren't just about equality; they were about recognizing the worth in every person. It's one of the greatest gifts she gave me, and it's a lesson I hope to pass on to my own children– that true equality comes from seeing the person before anything else, celebrating each person for their unique strengths and capabilities.

The evolution of roles should be about creating an environment where responsibilities are shared and valued equally, rather than diminishing their importance. When traditional roles are challenged, it is not about discarding these roles but about ensuring that all duties are fulfilled in a fair and equitable manner. This approach respects the significance of every role while adapting to new ways of distributing responsibilities.

Moreover, taking our responsibilities seriously is integral to the principles of equity. Everyone has a purpose and a duty that contributes to the overall well-being of their community. Avoiding these responsibilities under the guise of seeking equality undermines the essence of equity, which is about addressing and supporting each person's unique needs while fulfilling their roles with integrity.

Responsibility should be seen as a fundamental value that complements the ideals of equality and equity. Embracing our duties means understanding that every role has its significance and contributes to the collective good. Whether these duties are personal, familial, or professional, approaching them with commitment reflects a deeper understanding of our role in society and the impact we have on others.

By balancing our responsibilities with a commitment to fairness and respect, we create a more inclusive and equitable environment where every contribution is valued, and every duty is fulfilled with dedication and purpose.

My mother's wisdom continues to guide me, reminding me that empathy and understanding are crucial in our journey toward a more equitable world. Her lessons have left an indelible mark on my heart, shaping my values and actions. They serve as a constant reminder that while equality is essential, true justice and fairness come from recognizing and addressing the unique needs and challenges of every individual.

In honoring her memory, I strive to carry forward her legacy of empathy, equality, and equity in all aspects of my life. She taught me that being a better person means always striving to understand and support others, creating a world where everyone has the opportunity to thrive.

Corporate Learning: The Distinction Between Equality And Equity

"Diversity is being invited to the party. Inclusion is being asked to dance." - Verna Myers, an author, speaker, Vice President of Inclusion Strategy at Netflix

- **Tailored Treatment Over Generic Equality**: My mother's approach to treating individuals according to their unique worth rather than applying a one-size-fits-all standard is a powerful lesson for corporate settings. In business, it's essential to recognize that treating all employees the same (equality) does not account for their varied backgrounds, experiences, and challenges. Instead, equitable practices involve acknowledging these differences and tailoring support to meet individual needs.

- **Respect And Fairness**: My mother's respect for everyone, regardless of their social status, underscores the importance of fairness in the workplace. Respect should not be reserved for those in higher positions or those who fit a certain mold. Instead, every team member deserves to be treated with dignity and fairness. This means acknowledging their contributions and understanding their unique perspectives, and roles within the organization.

- **Beyond Surface-Level Equality**: Equality in the workplace often means equal access to opportunities, but equity goes a step further by addressing underlying barriers that may prevent some employees from succeeding. For example, if an employee is struggling due to personal challenges or systemic barriers, providing additional resources or support can help level the playing field. This could include mentorship programs, flexible work arrangements, or additional training.

- **Empathy As A Leadership Trait**: Empathy in leadership involves understanding and addressing the diverse needs and challenges of employees. My mother's ability to see humanity in everyone and respond with tailored support is a valuable lesson for leaders. Leaders should strive to understand their team members' individual circumstances and provide support that helps them succeed, rather than treating everyone the same regardless of their unique situations.

- **Creating A Supportive Culture**: Just as my mother created a nurturing environment at home, businesses should foster a culture where all employees feel valued and supported. This includes recognizing and celebrating individual strengths, understanding diverse needs, and providing opportunities for growth and development that are tailored to each person's circumstances.

- **Challenging Prejudices**: My mother's commitment to breaking down societal taboos and prejudices can be mirrored in corporate practices by challenging and addressing biases within the workplace. This involves creating an environment where open discussions about biases and inequalities are encouraged and implementing policies that promote inclusion and respect.

- **Leading By Example**: The way my mother embodied the principles of empathy, respect, and equity serves as a model for how leaders should act in the corporate world. Leading by example involves not just talking about equality and equity but demonstrating these values through actions and decisions that reflect a deep commitment to supporting every individual.

The lessons learned from my mother's approach to equality and equity offer a profound guide for creating a more inclusive and supportive workplace. By embracing the distinction between treating everyone the same and addressing individual needs, companies can build a more equitable environment where all employees have the opportunity to thrive. Her wisdom serves as a reminder that true equality is about recognizing and valuing the unique contributions of each person and providing the support needed to ensure everyone can reach their full potential.

I wish I had taken the time to truly listen to my mom and cherish her wisdom while I had the chance.

Your Notes: Reflections on Your Own Experience with Parents.

Chapter III
A Reflection Of Maya

"Common sense is not so common."

– François-Marie Arouet

The word 'Maya' has multiple origins, including Sanskrit, Greek, and Tupi.

Sanskrit: The word Māyā in Sanskrit means 'illusion' or 'magic.' It can also mean 'dream.' In Hindu Indian culture Laxmi, which means wealth in many contexts referred to as maya, which reminds that don't run to wealth it's all illusion.

Greek: The name Maya may be a variant of the Greek name Maia, which means 'mother.' Maia was the mother of Hermes and the eldest of the Pleiades in Greek and Roman mythology.

Tupi: In the Tupi language of southern Brazil, the word 'Maya' means 'mother'.'

Māori: In the Māori language, the name 'Maya' means 'courage' or 'bravery.'

Arabic: The Arabic name 'Mayya' is a variant of 'Maya.' It comes from the word May, which can mean 'good servant,' 'pretty woman,' or 'water.'

'Maya' may also refer to:

- The Maya civilization, an ancient civilization in Central America
- The Maya people, a modern Indigenous people of southern Mexico, Guatemala, and parts of Honduras
- The Mayan languages, the historical and modern languages of the Maya

The word 'Maya' can be seen as a multifaceted symbol that encompasses:

- The illusory nature of the material world: Recognizing that our perceptions are often distorted, and that true reality lies beyond the senses.
- The power of the divine feminine: Acknowledging the nurturing, creative, and courageous aspects of the feminine principle.

- The cyclical nature of existence: Understanding that life is a continuous process of birth, growth, and transformation.

These concepts emphasize transcending perceived reality to embrace a deeper, interconnected understanding of existence.

The word 'Maya' holds multiple meanings across cultures, from 'illusion' in Sanskrit to 'mother' in Tupi. However, its true meaning unfolds through personal experience, often beginning within the family. For me, understanding Maya has been a journey of self-discovery, deeply influenced by the wisdom and guidance of my mother.

In the old Asian Indian heritage, the wife of the gurukul head, the **brāhmaṇi**, played a vital role in shaping the character of children. In contrast, modern schooling, marked by transactional interactions between teachers and students, increasingly shifts the responsibility of imparting common sense and practical knowledge onto parents.

Teaching remains one of the noblest professions globally. However, excessive standardized testing, bureaucratic burdens, and limited autonomy have driven teachers to prioritize administrative tasks and test scores over student-centered learning. This transactional approach has narrowed curricula, increased stress, and reduced time for meaningful instruction. Additionally, inadequate resources and technology have further hindered personalized teaching.

The origins of the modern school system's factory-like structure trace back to the Industrial Revolution. Schools, inspired by the era's focus on efficiency and standardization, began grouping students by age, enforcing rigid schedules, and emphasizing rote learning and obedience over critical thinking. While this model seemed effective for the time, it neglected individual needs and stifled creativity.

Over recent decades, global competition and an increased focus on standardized testing have exacerbated this trend, placing academic achievement and test scores above holistic education. Consequently, schools today often overlook fostering creativity, individual growth, and social-emotional development in favor of efficiency and measurable outcomes.

In stark contrast, the Vedic age (approximately 1500–500 BCE) offered a holistic approach to education. The brāhmaṇi, the wife of a brāhmaṇa, held a significant yet understated role in the gurukul system. As students (brahmacharis) lived in their teacher's household, the brāhmaṇi complemented the guru's formal instruction by fostering an environment conducive to learning. She was far more than a caretaker; she actively shaped the students' character and moral foundation. This aligns with the duties of women as outlined in Manusmriti 9.28-29, which emphasize the pivotal role of a wife in upholding dharma within the household.

The brāhmaṇi ensured that students adhered to proper conduct, maintained cleanliness, lived disciplined lives, and key components of Vedic education. She guided them in practical tasks like managing household duties and participating in rituals, instilling values such as selflessness, devotion, and meticulousness. Her nurturing presence offered emotional and moral support, complementing the strict discipline of the guru. By embodying virtues like compassion, humility, and dedication to higher ideals, the brāhmaṇi served as a living example of dharmic living. The Rigveda (10.85) underscores the sanctity of a wife's role in fulfilling higher purposes, making her contribution indispensable.

Moreover, the Brahmani's knowledge of Vedic rituals and scriptures enabled her to enrich the spiritual education of students. Texts like the Brihadaranyaka Upanishad (2.4.1), which celebrates women scholars such as Gārgī, showcase the intellectual roles women played in the Vedic era. The Aitareya Brāhmaṇa (7.33) highlights the collaborative nature of rituals, where the wife's participation was critical to their success.

By assisting in these sacred ceremonies, the brāhmaṇi ensured students directly experienced the sanctity of Vedic practices. Her contributions extended beyond spiritual guidance; they fostered intellectual growth, moral integrity, and reverence for tradition. As documented in the Dharmasutras, particularly in texts such as the Gautama Dharmasutra and the Āpastamba Dharmasutra, which emphasize the wife's integral role in maintaining the household as a center of learning and virtue–her role exemplified collaborative teaching, with the household serving as a center of learning and virtue.

Reflecting on this ancient system, I find myself–though a data analytics professional who deeply values data-driven insights–realizing that not everything meaningful can or should be measured. I still remember the early years of school when writing didn't come easily to me. One of my elementary school teachers, frustrated by my spelling and grammar mistakes, would often punish me–sometimes by making me stand outside the classroom or remain standing through the lesson. It was humiliating, especially when my cousins and sisters were excelling academically and receiving praise.

Those experiences made me question my abilities and chipped away at my confidence. Yet, over time, I began to see that learning isn't always linear or measurable. Education, especially when it comes to nurturing character, creativity, and practical wisdom, cannot be reduced to test scores or numerical benchmarks.

This belief aligns closely with John Dewey's philosophy of experiential learning, which emphasizes the importance of fostering individuality, curiosity, and real-world problem-solving over standardized metrics. While I don't pretend to have all the answers, I do believe that if we focus only on what can be measured, we risk missing what truly matters. Our education systems must aim to recognize and develop the full range of human potential—not just the part that fits neatly into a spreadsheet.

In today's world, parents bear a greater responsibility to fill the gaps left by transactional schooling. They must impart values, common sense, and holistic knowledge. For me, my mother played an irreplaceable role in this regard, guiding me with wisdom and care, a modern-day reflection of the nurturing brāhmaṇi.

Life is a complex tapestry woven with threads of emotion and thought. While these feelings and ideas may not have a physical form, they profoundly influence our experiences and actions. As parents, we play a crucial role in guiding our children through this intricate landscape. My mother, in particular, was instrumental in imparting this wisdom to me. She consistently emphasized the importance of understanding and managing our emotions, as well as the power of positive thinking. Through her teachings, I learned to navigate the complexities of life with greater awareness and resilience.

In philosophical terms, maya is a concept from Hinduism, Buddhism, and other Eastern philosophies that refers to the illusion or appearance of the phenomenal world. It suggests that the world we perceive with our senses is not the ultimate reality but a distorted or temporary reflection. Maya represents the veil that clouds true understanding, keeping us from seeing the world as it truly is.

In Hinduism, maya is often associated with the divine power that creates and maintains the illusion of the material world. It is the force that causes the sense of duality, where we perceive ourselves as separate from the universe and other beings, rather than recognizing the underlying unity of existence.

In Buddhism, maya is also seen as the illusion of permanence and the misperception of self and external objects as real or lasting. It encourages practitioners to transcend the material world through mindfulness, meditation, and wisdom to understand the truth of impermanence and interconnectedness.

In Western thought, maya is not a term that is commonly used, but its closest equivalents might be related to the ideas of illusion, deception, or false perception. For example:

- Plato's Allegory of the Cave: In Western philosophy, particularly in Plato's writings, the concept of *maya* can be compared to the allegory of the cave, where prisoners are chained and only see shadows on the wall, mistaking them for reality. This allegory highlights the difference between appearances and the deeper, more profound truth of the world.
- Descartes' 'Cogito, ergo sum': René Descartes' exploration of doubt, where he questioned everything that could be doubted to find a foundation for certain knowledge, touches on themes similar to *maya* in that

our senses can deceive us, and only through reason can we come to understand what is truly real.

Mysticism and Esotericism: In mystical traditions, particularly in Western esotericism, *maya* can also be seen as the illusionary nature of the material world. Philosophers and mystics like *Plotinus* or *Gnostics* have reflected on the world as an illusion or veil, behind which lies the ultimate spiritual truth. They often discuss the necessity of transcending the mundane to experience spiritual awakening, echoing the sentiment of *maya* as an illusory barrier to enlightenment.

In Mexican and broader South American heritage, the concept of *maya* is often associated with the ancient **Maya civilization** rather than the philosophical or spiritual meanings found in Hinduism and Buddhism. However, the Maya people, who once thrived in what is now Mexico, Guatemala, Belize, Honduras, and El Salvador, have their own interpretations and cultural understandings that could be seen as related to illusions or the nature of reality in their worldview.

In Maya cosmology, the world was understood as a complex, multi-layered reality, with distinct realms that included the physical world, the underworld (Xibalba), and the heavens. These realms were deeply interconnected, and the boundaries between them were fluid. The Maya believed that the material world and the spiritual world were intricately intertwined, with events in one realm often influencing the other. This worldview may resonate with the concept of *maya* as an illusion or transient reality, where the physical world is but one aspect of existence. For the Maya, the spiritual realm, with its deities and ancestral connections, played a crucial role in daily life. Their understanding of life, death, and the cosmos involved an awareness of the impermanence of the material world.

In Maya and Aztec mythology, gods like Tezcatlipoca, the god of the night sky, were associated with themes of illusion and deception. Tezcatlipoca, often depicted with a smoking mirror, symbolized the trickster aspect of the world and represented the idea that reality is not always as it seems. While primarily an Aztec deity, the notion of deception through illusion was a concept that resonated across Mesoamerican cultures, including the Maya. It echoes the idea that the world we perceive may be fleeting or deceptive, much like the spiritual concept of *maya* as a veil hiding the true nature of existence.

The Maya's understanding of time further emphasizes this cyclical and impermanent worldview. Through their sophisticated calendar systems, such as the Haab (365-day solar calendar) and the Tzolk'in (260-day ritual calendar), the Maya viewed time not as a linear progression but as a repeating cycle. This cyclical perception reflects an understanding that life, death, and rebirth are part of an ongoing process. In this sense, time itself could be seen as an illusion, with the continuous repetition of events highlighting the transitory nature of reality.

Maya spirituality was deeply rooted in rituals and practices designed to maintain balance between the physical and spiritual realms. Ceremonies, bloodletting, and offerings were means of connecting with gods and ancestors, and they were intended to transcend the limitations of the material world. In this context, *maya* could be understood as the veil that obscures humanity's ability to fully connect with the divine or the cosmic order. Spiritual practices were viewed as a way to pierce this veil and recognize the true nature of existence, transcending the illusion of the physical world.

We often think and believe that civilizations across the world are vastly different—and on the surface, that may appear true. Cultures, languages, customs, and rituals may vary, giving the illusion of separation. But the deeper you go, the more you realize how similar we truly are. At the core of human experience lies the same longings, the same struggles, the same illusions. *Maya*—the veil of illusion, of appearances masking deeper truths—is one such thread that runs through all of us, across cultures and time.

The Convergence of Quantum Physics And Vedic Philosophy

The parallels between quantum physics and Vedic philosophy are striking. Both suggest that the reality we perceive is not the ultimate reality. Quantum physics, with its paradoxical nature, seems to support the idea of a deeper, underlying reality beyond the physical world. Similarly, Vedic philosophy posits that the material world is a manifestation of a higher, spiritual reality.

The concept of *maya* and the principles of quantum physics share some intriguing similarities, particularly in their treatment of the nature of reality and the distinction between appearance and underlying truth.

While the idea of *maya* originates in spiritual and philosophical contexts and quantum physics is a scientific framework, both challenge our conventional understanding of reality. They share an exploration of illusion, interconnectedness, and the limitations of human perception, inviting us to question what we see and experience and consider that deeper truths may lie beyond what we can immediately observe.

In both cases, reality appears to be much more complex and fluid than we tend to perceive, whether in spiritual or scientific terms.

While quantum physics and Vedic philosophy may seem worlds apart, they both point to the same fundamental truth: the nature of reality is far more complex and mysterious than we can imagine

I still remember all my discussions about *maya* with my mom, as though they happened just yesterday. Those conversations, so vivid and thoughtful, often left me questioning everything I thought I understood about reality. My exploration of the concept of *maya* across different cultures and time periods had reignited memories of one particular discussion with her, a memory entwined with her encounter with the renowned spiritual guru, Sri Sri Ravi Shankar.

My mom once had the fortune of meeting Sri Sri Ravi Shankar, the founder of the Art of Living Foundation, during one of his visits to Gaya—the city where she lived at the time. She attended a private session with him, accompanied by my father and a few close friends. It was during that gathering, she later told me over the phone, that she first heard his profound explanation of *maya*.

As she described it, Sri Sri Ravi Shankar explained that *maya* originates from Sanskrit and means "What can be measured." By that definition, anything that can be quantified–height, weight, distance, time, age–belongs to the realm of *maya*. In essence, *maya* is illusion: a fleeting, deceptive perception of reality.

I was struck by the elegance of that explanation, but it also left me unsettled.

Wanting to understand more, I asked her, "Then what is *not* maya?"

There was a brief pause on the line. Then, in her calm and familiar voice, she said, "What cannot be measured–joy, love, life itself."

Her words echoed in my mind long after the call ended. They didn't just answer my question–they invited me into a deeper reflection

What, then, is real if everything measurable is *maya*?

I went to bed that night consumed by thoughts of *maya* and its multifaceted interpretations. At times, I believed illusion was the core of *maya*, but now I was no longer certain. The more I tried to grasp its essence, the more it seemed to slip through my fingers.

The next morning, as I drove to the office, I knew I couldn't contain my questions any longer. I picked up the phone to call my mom, eager to confront her with my thoughts.

The moment she answered, I asked, "Mom, what exactly is *maya*?" She paused, and in that silence, I could almost hear her smile.

Finally, she said, "*Maya* is *maya*." Her cryptic response made me laugh.

"Mom, you've just confused me even more," I replied. "You'd better help me understand this."

She sighed and then asked, "Have you ever had a dream?"

"Of course," I replied.

"When you're dreaming, does it feel real to you?" she asked. I nodded, though she couldn't see me.

"Yes, in the dream it feels very real."

"And then what happens when you wake up?" she continued. "The dream fades, and you realize it wasn't real. Now tell me, have you ever wondered which life is real, the one in your dreams or the one you wake up to?"

I was silent for a moment, letting her words sink in. "Wow, Mom," I finally said. "You think you're helping me, but you're just adding to my confusion."

She laughed softly. “This dream analogy isn’t mine,” she admitted. “I borrowed it from the *Ashtavakra Gita*. It’s not the same as the *Bhagavad Gita* that most people know. The *Ashtavakra Gita* is a scripture that offers instructions for achieving self-realization. It teaches that our perception of reality is like a dream, an experience that feels real but isn’t the ultimate truth.”

Her explanation added another layer to my growing understanding of *maya*. It wasn’t just an illusion or something measurable; it was a challenge to discern what is truly real.

Was this life the reality, or was it another form of a dream, a transient experience that we wake from at some higher level of awareness? I couldn’t help but wonder if the very act of trying to define *maya* was an exercise in futility, a pursuit of a truth that lies beyond human comprehension.

And yet, this was the beauty of *maya*. It didn’t offer answers so much as it invited questions, pushing me to confront the boundaries of my understanding. Whether through the teachings of Sri Sri Ravi Shankar, the *Ashtavakra Gita*, or the dream-like wisdom of my mom, I was beginning to see that *maya* wasn’t a puzzle to be solved but a reality to be experienced, questioned, and ultimately transcended.

My curiosity resulted to searching a quiet a few verses reading, a few of verses from the *Ashtavakra Gita* that resonated deeply with the concept of *maya* and confusion:

On Illusion and Reality

"*You are not earth, water, fire, air, or space.*
You are not the body, nor are you the mind.
You are the witness, pure and alone.
Go happily." (*Ashtavakra Gita*, Chapter 1, Verse 3)

This verse strips away every label and association we have with ourselves. It calls us to realize that our true essence is beyond the physical and mental realms, that we are the eternal witness to all experiences.

In today's so-called modern world, where identities are so closely tied to possessions, social roles, and achievements, are we truly modern if we remain unaware of this deeper truth? The verse challenges us to rethink what progress means, suggesting that true evolution lies in understanding our timeless nature, not just in material advancements.

Illusion of Duality

"*The world appears as a shimmering mirage.*
To those with clear vision, it is nothing.

To the one who knows, it is neither real nor unreal."
(*Ashtavakra Gita*, Chapter 2, Verse 18)

This verse speaks to the paradoxical nature of reality. For the unenlightened, the world seems solid and absolute, but for the one with clear vision, it's a fleeting illusion. Modernity often traps us in the mirage of consumerism, appearances, and social validations. Are we really modern if we cannot discern between the ephemeral and the eternal? The verse invites us to pause and reflect on what holds true value in our lives.

On Letting Go of Confusion

"Bondage is imagining that you are a person.
Liberation is knowing you are not.
When this is clear, you are free."
(*Ashtavakra Gita*, Chapter 1, Verse 5)

This verse addresses the core of human confusion, our attachment to the idea of being a separate individual. We define ourselves by our roles, achievements, and failures, creating an illusion of bondage. In today's age of hyper-individualism and constant self-promotion, can we truly claim to be modern if we're still shackled by these illusions? True liberation lies in letting go of this false identification and recognizing our unity with the infinite.

These verses, though ancient, resonate profoundly with the challenges of our times. They remind us that modernity is not about technological advancement or societal progress alone. It is about transcending illusions, questioning our assumptions about reality, and awakening to our true nature. Whether through the wisdom of Sri Sri Ravi Shankar, my mother's insights, or the eternal teachings of the *Ashtavakra Gita*, I've come to see *maya* as an invitation, not to solve the puzzle of existence but to experience it with clarity, curiosity, and grace.

What I learned from her is that the truth we perceive is profoundly subjective, shaped by the lenses through which we view the world. Each of us carries a unique set of assumptions, beliefs, and values, all of which influence how we define and understand reality.

A simple question illustrates this beautifully: 'What is the sum of one plus one?' The instinctive answer is 'two,' but why do we accept this so readily? It is because we have been taught to adhere to a specific mathematical framework that defines one and one as equaling two. Yet, in another framework, perhaps a symbolic or conceptual one, this equation might yield a different result entirely.

Truth, then, is not absolute. It is a construct that emerges from the systems we create and the contexts we inhabit. Cultural traditions, societal norms, and personal experiences all act as filters, coloring our understanding of what is real and what is not. In essence, we live within a tapestry of interconnected perceptions, where what we believe to be true is often just a reflection of the standards we've chosen, or been conditioned, to accept.

Maya is the perfect embodiment of this concept. At its core, *maya* represents the veil of illusion, the idea that what we see and believe may not be the ultimate truth. It invites us to question the frameworks we rely on and consider that the 'truths' we hold might only be one version of reality, rather than an immutable fact. Through this lens, I have come to appreciate the complexities of perspective, the art of unlearning, and the beauty of questioning what we think we know.

However, while *maya* urges us to question our perceptions, we must also navigate a world increasingly shaped by misinformation and disinformation. These terms, though they describe phenomena that have existed for centuries, have taken on heightened relevance in today's hyper-connected society.

Misinformation refers to false or misleading information that is spread unintentionally. Historically, misinformation often traveled through rumors, gossip, and word-of-mouth. With the advent of print media, newspapers and magazines became powerful tools for spreading both accurate and inaccurate information. Disinformation, by contrast, refers to deliberately false information spread with the intent of deceiving or manipulate. From wartime propaganda in World War I and II to modern social media campaigns, disinformation has been used as a weapon to shape opinions and influence outcomes.

Today, social media platforms amplify the challenges of disinformation in ways we couldn't have imagined a few decades ago. The pursuit of likes, views, and followers has created an environment where truth often takes a backseat to virality. This cultural shift poses new challenges for everyone, especially parents.

As a child growing up in the 1980s in India, punishment often meant a 'time out.' It was a simple yet effective method that encouraged self-reflection. I remember being sent to my room to think about my actions, and it served as a quiet space for introspection. But as a parent today, I find that giving kids a 'time out' for reflection is almost impossible. Unlike in my childhood, where solitude often meant disconnecting from the world, children today are more connected in their rooms than they are in the family-living area. Technology, for all its benefits, has blurred the boundaries between reflection and distraction.

Even when children are sent to their rooms, they're not truly alone. Laptops for homework, cloud-based assignments, and virtual classrooms make the internet an essential part of their daily lives. Add to this the presence of voice assistants like Siri, Alexa, and Google, and the concept of 'alone time' has become almost obsolete. The world is always within reach, and as parents, we must navigate this new reality carefully.

During our conversations, my mother often emphasized that parenthood is a complex and ever-changing responsibility. She stressed that it is unfair to measure or compare parenting across generations. Her experiences as a parent were shaped by a world vastly different from the one I am raising my children in. The norms, expectations, and challenges we face are unique to our respective times, and attempting to compare them only creates unrealistic standards.

Her wisdom reminded me that the essence of parenthood lies not in adhering to fixed ideals but in adapting to the evolving needs of our children and the world they inhabit. As I reflect on these lessons, I realize that *maya* is not just an abstract concept about illusion and reality, it is also a lens through which we can better understand the fluidity of life, the shifting nature of truth, and the importance of embracing the present with clarity and compassion.

In today's so-called modern world, where progress is often equated with technological advancement, it is worth asking: Are we truly modern? We have conquered space, connected the globe, and unlocked the secrets of the human genome. Yet, as we navigate a world inundated with information, both true and false, the question remains: Have we evolved in our ability to discern what truly matters? Modernity, perhaps, is not about the tools we use but the wisdom with which we use them. It is not about accumulating knowledge but about understanding ourselves and the world with greater depth and humility.

In this sense, *maya* is more relevant than ever. It challenges us to look beyond the surface, to question the truths we take for granted, and to seek a deeper understanding of reality. And in doing so, it reminds us that the journey of self-discovery is timeless, transcending the boundaries of culture, technology, and time itself.

Lessons From Maya: Insights For The Corporate World

As I reflect on the concept of Maya and the wisdom imparted by my mother, it's clear that the ancient teachings resonate deeply, even in the fast-paced, target-driven environments of today's corporate world. Here are some key takeaways that bridge the timeless with the modern:

- **Leadership Beyond Metrics**
  Just as the brāhmaṇi nurtured students in the gurukul system, effective leaders must inspire beyond targets and deadlines. True leadership fosters ethical behavior, emotional intelligence, and the personal growth of each team member.

- **The Danger Of Over-Standardization**
  Like the factory-style education model, workplaces overly focused on rigid KPIs risk stifling creativity and individuality. Innovation thrives when organizations balance structure with freedom of thought.

- **Questioning Assumptions**
  Maya teaches us to challenge perceived realities. In the workplace, this means questioning biases, avoiding hasty conclusions, and relying on both intuition and evidence to make informed decisions.

- **Adaptability Is Key**
  Parenthood, and leadership, requires adapting to evolving circumstances. Leaders must remain flexible, learning and

recalibrating as they navigate changing markets, technologies, and team dynamics.

- **Value Emotional And Social Intelligence**
  The brāhmaṇi's role underscores the importance of emotional guidance. In the corporate context, empathy and strong interpersonal skills foster collaboration and resolve conflicts effectively.

- **The Power Of Reflection**
  Reflection, as illuminated by Maya, is crucial. Taking time to step back and analyze successes, failures, and strategies ensures continual growth and alignment with long-term goals.

- **Focusing On The Bigger Picture**
  Maya reminds us of the impermanence of fleeting trends. Corporate leaders must prioritize sustainable growth and long-term vision over short-term gains.

- **Ethics As The Cornerstone**
  The spiritual and moral guidance from the Vedic era highlights the importance of integrity. In the corporate world, ethical practices are the bedrock of trust and enduring success.

- **Modernity Lies In Awareness**
  True progress isn't in technological advancements alone but in the wisdom with which we use them. Being mindful of the human element ensures that modernity serves a higher purpose.

- **Maya As A Catalyst For Growth**
  Ultimately, Maya invites us to see beyond illusions, embrace uncertainty, and grow through questioning. The workplace, much like life, is a landscape of shifting truths, urging us to stay curious and adaptable.

As I recall my mother's wisdom, these lessons remind me that Maya isn't just an abstract concept but a guide to navigating both life and work with clarity, compassion, and a relentless pursuit of what truly matters.

I wish I had taken the time to truly listen to my mom and cherish her wisdom while I had the chance.

Your Notes: Reflections on Your Own Experience with Parents.

Chapter IV
Respect

अमानित्वं अदंभित्वं अहिंसा क्षणन्तिर आर्जवं
आचार्योपासनां शौकं स्थिरं आत्मविनिग्रहः

*"amānitvam adambhitvam ahiṁsā kṣāntir ārjavam
ācāryopāsanaṁ śaucaṁ sthairyam ātmavinigrahaḥ"*

Bhagavad Gita, Chapter 13, *Verse* 8

This verse lists qualities that are esteemed in a person of spiritual knowledge. Among these qualities are humility (amānitvam) and pride lessness (adambhitvam), which are closely related to respect.

Respect, in this context, involves recognizing the value of others without letting pride or ego get in the way. It also includes approaching a teacher or parents with reverence (ācāryopāsanaṁ), indicating a deep respect for those who impart wisdom.

One morning, I woke up to a flurry of WhatsApp notifications from our middle school friends' group chat. Usually, the conversations were a mix of forwarded messages, inside jokes, and the kind of banter that rarely held any lasting relevance. But that day, one message stood out and caught my eye:

"Wisdom isn't just about knowing what to say or do; it's about understanding when to say or do it. True wisdom lies in recognizing the value of patience, learning from every experience, and having the courage to make thoughtful choices"

I read the message twice, letting the words sink in. It wasn't that I didn't understand it rather it stirred something deep within me. It reminded me of my mother and the countless times she had shared her wisdom with me in her gentle yet firm way. She had a way of weaving her life lessons into everyday moments, often catching me off guard with her insight. Whether it was while she was cooking in the kitchen or knitting on the porch, she always found the right moment to teach me something valuable.

As I read that message, I could almost hear her voice, filled with a mix of warmth and sternness, telling me things I often shrugged off as a teenager. I realized how much I missed those moments, her soft laughter, her words of encouragement, and even her occasional scoldings that were always meant to guide me.

If only I had listened more closely to her words while she was still here, I thought, maybe I would have been a wiser, better person today. In that moment, I felt an overwhelming sense of longing for her presence. She had always been my compass, guiding me through life's challenges with her wisdom and love. Now, all I had were her memories and the lessons she left behind.

As we grew up, a few phrases frequently echoed in our home, repeated often by our mother: 'Respect is not asked for; it's earned,' 'Let it go' and 'It will be ok.' At the time, these sayings felt more like a frustrating way for her to end a conversation. I often found them infuriating, especially when I wanted to argue my point or hold on to my grievances. But as I reflect on those words now, I realize how deeply they shaped my character over the years.

Her words have become guiding principles in my life, teaching me that respect must be earned through genuine actions and integrity. They also remind me of the importance of letting go of grudges and negativity, allowing me to move forward with a clearer mind and heart. What once felt like a dismissive end to a discussion has, over time, become the foundation of my approach to life and relationships.

Mummy, reflecting on your teachings about equality and respect, I've come to understand that they have shaped me in profound ways. Your lessons have taught me the importance of treating everyone fairly and with kindness, which I'm grateful for. However, I also realize that this can be a double-edged sword. In my effort to respect and care for others, I sometimes forget to take care of myself. It's a delicate balance, ensuring that I stand up for my own needs while also being considerate of others. I'm learning that respecting myself is just as important as respecting those around me. Although I will accept that I am still not spiritually so enlightened that I can understand what is and is not required to live a fulfilling life.

One morning, while driving to the office as usual, I was on the phone with my mom. I confided in her, "No one respects me in our extended family." I expected her to reassure me, to say something like, 'It's not like that.'

But to my surprise, she didn't. Instead, she asked, "Why do you think people will respect you?"

Taken aback, I replied, "Because I'm a good person. I'm humble..." My voice trailed off as I searched for the right words.

Her response was grounded in the kind of practicality she'd always had. "It's not that simple," she explained. "Respect is a long process. At first, people might respect you for your job title, or for how much money you have. Right now, you have a good job, but it's hard to explain, and no one in the extended family directly benefits from it. And let's face it, you're not in a position to help them financially."

I felt a flash of frustration and said, "Then your life lesson that 'Respect is earned' is wrong."

She paused, and her voice softened. "It's not wrong," she said gently, "but it's not so straightforward either. Life will teach you that, over time."

That day, the word 'respect' consumed my thoughts. It lingered in my mind, weaving through every task I attempted to focus on. The conversation with my mom replayed over and over. I couldn't shake the discomfort her bluntness had caused me. What did she mean when she said it wasn't so simple?

At the time, I was in my early 30s, old enough to handle my responsibilities, but still not quite seasoned enough to fully grasp the wheels of life and all its complexities. I had thought I understood respect. I believed that by being a good person, by taking care of my duties, and by being humble, I had done enough to earn it. But my mom's words suggested otherwise.

I found myself searching for answers, something to ground my emotions and clarify what felt like an unexpected blow to my self-worth. I even turned to Google, typing 'respect' into the search bar. The Oxford Dictionary definition popped up, crisp and clear– 'a strong feeling of approval of somebody or something because of their good qualities or achievements.'

The words stared back at me, and I realized that they mirrored much of what my mom had said. Respect, as the dictionary defined it, wasn't simply about being good or humble, which were qualities I had always considered essential. The definition emphasized achievements, the very thing my mom had pointed out. Respect, at least in today's world, seemed to hinge more on tangible accomplishments, things others could see or measure, especially in a materialistic, transactional society where even relationships sometimes felt like negotiations of value.

As I reflected, I began to see that she wasn't dismissing my goodness or humility. She wasn't saying those qualities didn't matter. What she was telling me was that they weren't enough on their own, at least not in the immediate sense. Respect, in her eyes, was a longer process, one built slowly over time. It wasn't just about having good intentions but about translating those intentions into actions that could be seen and felt by others.

But in that moment, I wasn't ready to confront the complexity of it all. I didn't want to accept that my job or financial situation–things that often felt disconnected from my true self–could shape how others saw me. I just wanted to hold on to the comforting belief that being a good person should be enough.

So, to quiet the dissonance in my mind and get back to the tasks at hand, I made a mental excuse: Mom must have been in a bad mood. Or maybe she was just being too direct, as she sometimes could be when she was trying to prove a point. I tried to move on, pushing the discomfort aside, as if attributing her bluntness to a momentary lapse in gentleness could make the whole conversation less significant.

But even as I dove back to work, a part of me knew that what she'd said wasn't born out of a bad mood or momentary frustration. It was born out of experience. My mom had lived long enough, and with a diversity of experiences in various circumstances, to know that respect was something earned, not just by being good, but by navigating the complexities of life. She understood that earning respect wasn't always about moral high ground alone. It was about showing the world your value in ways they could understand and recognize, especially in a world that often only sees what it can measure.

Her life had taught her that respect could look different in different contexts: in a family, it might come from responsibility and care; in society, it could stem from achievements or influence; and in personal relationships, it might grow from trust and understanding.

My mom, my unwavering cheerleader, didn't say what I was bracing for that day. The next morning, I made a brief call, gave her a quick, "Everything's fine," and said I had a work call to take. It had become my go-to tactic for avoiding deeper conversations when I wasn't in the mood. But I knew my mom saw through it. She always did.

A few days later, during one of our routine chats, she casually brought up some political news, which was typical. But then, she shifted the conversation to Rahul Gandhi, the grandson of Indira Gandhi, India's first woman prime minister, and son of Rajiv Gandhi, both of whom had earned their respect and legacies. Her point was clear. She wanted me to see that people respect Rahul because of where he comes from, his family, his heritage. "Respect," she said, "can be something you inherit. It's passed down."

I shrugged her off, as usual. "That might work for someone like him or royalty," I said. "Rahul Gandhi, or even Queen Elizabeth and Prince Charles, they get respect because of the family they were born into, not because of who they are. It's the monarchy, Mom. That's not how it works for regular people like us. We don't get to inherit respect; we have to earn it."

But my mom, with her steady patience, didn't let it go. "You think it's just about titles, but it's not," she replied. "Look at Queen Elizabeth. She was respected not because she was a monarch, but because she carried herself with a certain dignity, a sense of duty. Even Prince Charles, who's been criticized for years, still commands a certain respect because of the legacy he represents, not just the title."

She paused, then added, "But not everyone who inherits a legacy holds onto it. Take Aurangzeb, the Mughal emperor. His father, Shah Jahan, was respected as the builder of the Taj Mahal and for his reign. Yet Aurangzeb, despite inheriting the powerful Mughal throne, became despised for his intolerance and harsh rule. He lost the respect his family had built over generations because of his actions."

I stopped for a moment, considering her words. She was making a connection I hadn't thought about that respect isn't just about what you earn yourself, but how you handle the legacy you inherit. And sometimes, through your own deeds, you can lose that respect, no matter where you come from.

Her point was starting to sink in, even though I wasn't quite ready to acknowledge it. Maybe respect is a balance of inheritance and personal responsibility, something you can build on or throw away.

Her words hit me deeply, a truth so simple yet profound. It felt like my biggest cheerleader had just laid out the reality I needed to hear. Somehow, her insight brought me a sense of peace. In that moment, I realized I had been chasing respect in all the wrong ways, seeking external validation instead of focusing inward. That conversation shifted something in me. I stopped overthinking and striving to be seen in a certain way by others. Instead, I felt relief, satisfaction, and, most importantly, happiness in just being.

Mom and I couldn't seem to let go of this respect topic. For weeks, it kept surfacing in our conversations, each time with new questions and insights.

One morning, I shared my frustration with her. “Sometimes, no matter how much I do–whether it’s helping someone financially, putting in extra effort, or going out of my way–it doesn’t feel like it’s noticed. I thought my actions alone would earn respect, but it’s often the opposite. It’s like my effort is invisible.”

She listened quietly; her silence filled with thoughtfulness. Then she said, “That’s because respect is rarely shaped by actions alone. It’s also tied to the relationships, histories, and unspoken bonds people already have. Sometimes, those unseen ties matter more than what you do in the moment.”

Her words stayed with me. They reminded me that respect isn’t only something you earn–it’s something that flows through the networks of trust and legacy we’re part of. Actions matter, yes, but so does the ground you’re standing on.

The topic of respect lingered in my mind longer than I expected. The very next morning, during a call with Mom, I dove right in, skipping the usual small talk. “Now I see why people sometimes hold me in such regard,” I said thoughtfully.

Mom, always patient, asked simply, “Why?”

"Well," I began, "first, I had the privilege of being raised by you and Papa—two people whose character and values are admired by everyone who knows them. And then, there's Papa's reputation. His integrity, his hard work, and the respect he earned in the extended family and community still carry weight. Even though I'm far from India and not in a government or high-profile role, I feel like a part of that respect flows to me. It's as if I'm standing on the sturdy shoulders of the life you both built."

I smiled as I said it, and Mom chuckled quietly before replying, "It's never just one thing, but you're not far off."

Her words felt like a gentle affirmation, a moment of clarity I wanted to hold onto. I shifted the conversation quickly, not wanting to dwell too long on this newfound insight. Still, I felt a quiet thrill—a lightness—as if I'd just unraveled a knot I hadn't realized was there.

In many ways, parents are a child's first teachers, shaping their understanding of respect long before the world has a chance to influence them. My mom often reminded me that respect begins at home, not just in how we speak or act, but in the way we observe and value those around us. She modeled this every day through her words and actions, showing me how to treat others with kindness, empathy, and fairness. Like a teacher, she taught through example, guiding me to understand that respect isn't just about politeness, it's about recognizing the worth of every individual, including myself. In her own way, she also played the role of a wise leader, balancing authority with love and creating a sense of legacy by passing down values that tied us to our roots.

It was the fall of 2013, the day after Halloween. I remember because the day started on a bad note but somehow ended on a peaceful one. As usual, I was on a call with my mom while heading to the office. At the time, we had two infants at home, and like any other marriage, mine had its own set of challenges. Normally, I avoid discussing my marriage life with her, but that day, frustration got the better of me.

"Marriage is such an overrated concept," I blurted out. "I don't even know why society insists on it. If raising kids is the goal, there are plenty of ways to do that without tying people together in this exhausting arrangement!"

I was on a roll. "Honestly, I think Plato had a point. Marriage and child-rearing should just be the government's responsibility."

Mom stayed silent, letting me vent. Once I finally stopped babbling, she calmly asked, "What happened?"

"I'm tired," I admitted. "No matter what I do, I feel like I can't make my wife happy. Sometimes, I think it'd be easier to just walk away."

She sighed. "Just be cool and be realistic."

But I wasn't in the mood for calm wisdom. "Mom, your time was different!" I snapped. "Papa is lucky you are his wife. Relationships back then were simpler. You didn't have to deal with half the stuff we do now. So tell me, how did you manage your marriage?"

She chuckled. "Marriage isn't a bed of roses. And it's definitely not a Karan Johar movie."

That made me pause. "Wait, so now we're blaming Bollywood?"

"Not blaming," she said. "Just pointing out that Karan Johar grew up in a world where money wasn't an issue. He made glossy, dreamy romances because he could afford to. Real life isn't like that—it's full of ups and downs, and you have to accept what you have and keep moving forward."

I sighed. "Okay, so what does a perfect marriage mean to you?"

She didn't hesitate. "It's subjective. But to me, a good marriage is built on trust and the ability to accept each other's shortcomings—because no one is perfect, and no relationship ever will be."

I let that sink in. I had been looking for some grand, complex answer—maybe even an escape route—but Mom, in her usual way, had cut straight to the heart of it.

Marriage wasn't about finding the perfect partner. It was about learning to ride the waves together, even when the tide was rough. And maybe, just maybe, that was enough.

Mom used to say that the family is the first place where we learn how respect operates, how to give it, how to earn it, and how it shapes relationships. Whether through stories, conversations, or her handling of life's challenges, she instilled in me the importance of respecting others' efforts, roles, and perspectives. She also emphasized self-respect as the foundation of it all, reminding me that we can only truly respect others when we value ourselves. Her teachings weren't limited to our family; they extended to the wider world, where respect meant embracing diversity and appreciating people's unique contributions. In her, I saw the perfect blend of a teacher's wisdom and a queen's grace, quiet yet powerful lessons that stayed with me long after the words were spoken.

Family is the first institute we belong to, and marriage is no different, it's an institution that teaches us commitment, understanding, tolerance and respect. To truly honor marriage as a relationship, we must see it as something beyond individual egos. Too often, in the pursuit of having it all, we overlook the respect owed to the relationships that anchor us, whether it's with our partner, parents, or children. In any relationship, acceptance matters far more than expectations. When we learn to embrace the people, we love as they are, rather than shaping them to meet our ideals, we cultivate a deeper and more enduring respect.

Buddha, born as Siddhartha Gautama in ancient India, was a prince who renounced his royal life in search of a deeper truth about human suffering. Through years of meditation and self-discovery, he attained enlightenment under the Bodhi tree in Gaya, Bihar, incidentally, the same place where I was born. While he found the ultimate truth of life and liberation, I'm still trying to figure out how to make sense of my in-laws and others. His teachings, which form the foundation of Buddhism, are centered around compassion, self-awareness, and the pursuit of inner peace.

Buddha often taught that knowing yourself is the key to building harmonious relationships. He believed that self-awareness allows us to let go of ego and find inner peace. When we turn inward to understand our true selves, we uncover the strength to accept others as they are, without imposing our expectations or seeking external validation. As he said in the Dhammapada, 'You yourself, as much as anybody in the entire universe, deserve your love and affection.'

This self-understanding helps us see the interconnectedness of all beings and fosters genuine respect. In today's world, where social media thrives on 'likes' and external applause, this wisdom feels more relevant than ever. True respect within a relationship doesn't need an audience; it grows in private moments of understanding, compromise, and trust. By focusing on our inner selves and finding contentment within, we can nurture relationships built on genuine acceptance, gratitude, and humility.

It was 2019, during India's general elections. Like many countries, India had become deeply divided in its political choices, perhaps polarized is a better word. One morning, I was on a call with my mom when our conversation drifted to politics.

"It's good that the country is divided," I said casually. "At least the ruling party has a clear mandate."

She was silent for a moment before responding. “Having two sides is fine, but the problem isn’t just division, it’s how far apart the sides have drifted.”

I frowned. “But isn’t it natural for people to have strong opinions?”

She sighed. “It is but let me explain it differently. Imagine a wooden plank balancing on a fulcrum. To stay steady, it needs to find its center of gravity. You can do that in multiple ways, or by evenly distributing weight on both sides or by placing all the weight at the extreme edges.” She paused. “But when all the weight is at the edges, the pressure builds, and eventually, the plank snaps.”

I leaned back, letting her words sink in.

“Democracy is the same,” she continued. “Differences are natural, even necessary. But when people stop listening to each other, when they refuse to find common ground, the system weakens. True balance isn’t about making everyone agree, it’s about making space for different views without turning them into battle lines.”

I said, “So, respect keeps the plank from breaking?”

She laughed. “Exactly. If we can respect each other’s opinions, even when we disagree, we hold everything together.”

That morning, I realized respect isn't just about politeness, it's about preserving the very foundation of our unity.

My definition or rather better to say, me learning about respect. Respect is a recognition that is earned over time, not just through good intentions and personal virtues, but through actions that demonstrate value to others. It is a balance between who you are as a person, your character, humility, and integrity, and what you contribute to the world through your achievements and tangible efforts.

In a society where relationships can often feel transactional, respect comes when people see not only your qualities but also how those qualities manifest in ways that benefit or resonate with them.

However, respect is also deeply personal. Like beauty, it starts with how one holds themselves, rooted in self-care and self-worth. True respect begins with respecting yourself. Before you can expect it from others, you must value your own journey. It's not just a reflection of what others think or feel about you, but a reflection of how you view yourself. In this way, respect is more of a journey than a destination, a process that grows over time as you build both internal strength and external contributions.

Corporate Respect

***"It is not sufficient to be worthy of respect in order to be respected."* – Alfred Nobel**

- **The Importance Of Legacy In Leadership:** Just as history illustrates that respect is earned through consistent actions, the corporate world mirrors this truth in leadership. A leader's legacy is not built by authority alone but by the fairness, inclusivity, and empowerment they bring to their teams. True respect stems from decisions that inspire trust and elevate others, reflecting the enduring value of legacy.
- **Mutual Respect Across Generations In The Workplace:** The dynamic of respect between generations, akin to the relationship between seasoned mentors and eager learners, underscores the importance of mutual growth. As younger professionals bring fresh ideas and experienced leaders provide invaluable guidance, respect flourishes when both sides listen, learn, and evolve together. Corporate success lies in fostering this symbiosis.
- **Walking The Fine Line Between Respect And Fear:** History reveals the stark contrast

between leaders who are respected and those merely feared. In corporate settings, this distinction determines the longevity of influence. A leader who earns respect through integrity, empathy, and vision cultivates loyalty and innovation, whereas fear-driven authority fades, leaving behind discontent and stagnation.

- **Empathy As A Skill In Corporate Respect:** Empathy stands as the cornerstone of respect, transcending hierarchical boundaries. Just as understanding others' experiences fosters deeper connections in life, the corporate world thrives when managers grasp the challenges and aspirations of their teams. This understanding creates an environment where respect is mutual and productivity flourishes.

- **Respect As A Reflection Of Actions:** Respect is not demanded but earned, as actions speak louder than words. A company's reputation, and by extension, its respectability, is shaped by how it treats employees, customers, and stakeholders. Similarly, employees gain respect through their dedication, collaboration, and resilience, embodying the principle that respect is the byproduct of meaningful contributions.

- **Acknowledging The Complexity Of Earning Respect:** The transient nature of respect reminds us that it must be cultivated with care and vigilance. In corporate culture, respect hinges on the consistency of values and actions. A company celebrated for innovation may lose its esteem if it disregards ethical practices, just as a leader may falter if they stray from their principles.
- **Respect Beyond Titles And Roles:** Respect transcends titles, affirming that it is rooted in character and action. In the corporate world, respect belongs equally to the intern who contributes novel ideas, the manager who shields their team, and the CEO who admits mistakes. It is the authenticity of these actions that define respect, reminding us that legacy is not confined to position but to purpose.

I wish I had taken the time to truly listen to my mom and cherish her wisdom while I had the chance.

Your Notes: Reflections on Your Own Experience with Parents.

Chapter V
Nurture The Resources

"Truly rich are those who enjoy what they have"

– The Yiddish proverb

I was fortunate that I was born into a well-to-do family, where education and well-being were always prioritized. On reflection, I can say that we, brothers, sisters, and cousins, were well-born with silver spoons. However, the silver spoon doesn't mean that we had an abundance of money; rather, it was that we had abundance in other forms, abundance in opportunities, in love, in education, and in the values that were instilled in us.

In many ways, we were rich in resources that, though not always material, shaped our lives in profound ways. These resources were not always visible in the form of wealth or possessions, but in the intangible gifts we were given–the freedom to explore, the chance to learn, the encouragement to grow, and the unwavering support of family. It was this kind of abundance that truly defined our lives.

As a reminder, prior to the early 1990s, India operated under a highly regulated and closed economy. This restrictive environment significantly impacted resource availability, limited access to foreign goods, and constrained the development of a modern financial system. Credit cards were virtually non-existent, and the availability of imported goods was severely restricted due to high tariffs and trade barriers. While India embarked on significant economic liberalization in 1991, the benefits of these reforms took longer to reach smaller towns like Gaya, Bihar, due to geographical and infrastructural limitations.

Of course! I'll integrate the ideas of mother's resource management with the symbolic and practical aspects of the cow in the narration.

The first economics professor I ever interacted with was my mom. She never formally studied economics, but she was a master at managing and distributing limited resources. Economics, at its core, is about making choices that maximize well-being despite scarcity. While the common focus often centers around money, my mom showed me early on that real wealth lies in how we manage all the resources at our disposal, our time, our relationships, our skills, and our capacity to contribute.

Growing up, I watched my mom carefully navigate the challenges that come with limited financial resources, and she made those choices with grace and wisdom. One of the most striking lessons she imparted was how to stretch every rupee/dollar without compromising on the essentials. Every month, she would sit down, assess the family's budget, and then plan the grocery shopping. It wasn't about how much money we had, but about how she could make the most out of what we did have. Grocery shopping was an art form for her; she would plan meals for the entire month, creating lists of necessities, estimating costs, and ensuring that each purchase was a thoughtful decision.

Through her actions, I learned that managing resources isn't just about money. It's about making thoughtful choices, being mindful of how we use what we have, and understanding that true wealth is the capacity to live with intention and care. In the face of scarcity, my mom showed me that we have the power to create abundance in every area of our lives.

This principle of nurturing resources is mirrored in the broader philosophy of life. For instance, consider the significance of the cow in various traditions, including Hinduism. The cow, known as 'dhenuḥ,' is more than just a creature; it's a symbol of fertility, wealth, and life itself. It was the first domesticated animal, offering not just sustenance but a range of valuable resources: milk, ghee (clarified butter), gomutra (urine), and gomaya (dung). Each of these products plays an essential role in nurturing life in different ways.

- **Milk**: It's a fundamental source of nutrition, offering growth and health benefits, while Ayurveda suggests it can enhance radiation resistance and brain cell regeneration.
- **Ghee (Clarified Butter)**: Highly valued in Ayurveda for its healing properties and effectiveness in treating various ailments.
- **Gomutra (Urine)**: Used for medicinal purposes, with properties that include anti-cancer, anti-bacterial, and immune-boosting effects.
- **Gomaya (Dung)**: Provides natural nutrients for plants, rejuvenating the soil and promoting organic farming practices. It's a reminder of the importance of natural resources in sustaining life and the earth.

The cow's various gifts reflect a broader philosophy of nurturing resources that are essential to our lives. Just as my mom carefully managed our household resources to create stability and abundance, these natural resources teach us about the value of mindful stewardship. It's about understanding that true wealth extends beyond financial assets; it's about recognizing and caring for all forms of resources, whether they are tangible, like food and fuel, or intangible, like knowledge, relationships, and the environment.

There are certain conversations and moments that resonate with you no matter how much time has passed. For me, one such memory dates to when I was in the 7th grade, a milestone of sorts, as it was the year I got my first pair of jeans. It wasn't because of any financial constraints or a lack of opportunity; it was simply that owning a pair of jeans hadn't been a necessity until then.

I can still picture those jeans vividly. They were a deep shade of blue, with a texture that was both sturdy and soft, a fabric that seemed to promise adventure. What made them truly unforgettable, though, was the design on the back right pocket. It wasn't like any ordinary pocket. Instead, it featured an intricate pattern of half-centimeter strips that resembled a mat weave. These strips were carefully arranged, forming a crisscrossing texture over a pocket that measured about 3 by 4 inches.

That small detail, the unique weave of that pocket, felt like something special, something uniquely mine. It wasn't just a piece of clothing; it was a symbol of something new, something personal. Even now, when I think back to that time, I smile at the memory of those jeans and how they made me feel. They weren't just fabric and thread; they were part of a moment in my life that felt like stepping into something bigger, something a little more grown-up.

One of my vivid memories takes me back to grade 5th, to the day we bought my first bicycle. The price of it is etched in my mind, Rs (INR) 550. Adjusted for today's value, it would be about Rs 6000, roughly equivalent to USD 70. The journey to owning and riding that bicycle wasn't ordinary. Long before I had one of my own, I had already mastered the art of balancing and pedaling. Ironically, my lessons began while helping my elder sister learn to ride. No one took me by the hand to teach me. Instead, it was sheer determination and a burning desire to ride that made me learn on my own.

A similar story unfolded when it came to driving a car. No formal lessons, no guiding hands. By the time I was in the 9th grade, it became my responsibility to start the car every three or four days to keep the battery from discharging. My father seldom drove it, as he preferred his trusty two-wheeler for daily commutes. The car, a symbol of family outings, stood mostly unused, a relic for occasional journeys. But those family outings were rare. Instead, our lives revolved around a constant stream of cousins and guests, filling our home with laughter and conversations that made outings unnecessary.

These small acts, learning to ride a bicycle, starting the car, weren't just chores or hobbies. They were my early lessons in self-reliance, curiosity, and the quiet determination to take charge, even in the absence of guidance.

My mother had a unique approach to teaching life lessons, an 'inductive' method, as I like to call it. She fostered independent exploration by supporting my endeavors and encouraging me to figure things out on my own. We shared an unspoken agreement– if I ever made a mistake, she would be the first to know.

I vividly recall an incident during high school when I skipped a class to watch a movie. Nervously, I confessed to my mother, fully expecting a scolding. To my astonishment, she didn't reprimand me. Instead, she asked, "How was the movie?" Then, with her usual calm demeanor, she reminded me not to make it a habit and to ensure my studies remained a priority.

Reflecting on her parenting style, I realize she was teaching us, my siblings and me, the value of managing resources, particularly time. She understood my father's busy schedule meant he couldn't teach my sister to ride a bike, so she devised a solution that aligned with our unique learning styles. She recognized that conventional methods, like learning from books or structured training, didn't work well for me. Whether this was due to a cognitive challenge or superiority didn't matter. What mattered was creating the best possible environment for me to learn.

At the core of her method was trust. She trusted me, which is why she chose not to scold but to listen. That trust allowed me to take risks, knowing that mistakes wouldn't be met with harsh judgment but rather understanding and guidance. It gave me the courage to step outside my comfort zone, try new things, and learn from both successes and failures. Her trust became the foundation of my self-reliance and growth, shaping me into someone who values responsibility, independence, and the balance between taking risks and staying accountable.

Coming back to the story of buying my first bicycle, what might seem like a minor event was, in fact, a defining moment. I still remember the effort it made to convince my parents. It wasn't a simple request; it required months of persistence and countless explanations about why I needed my own bicycle. This early experience of having to present reasonable arguments shaped my thinking profoundly.

Looking back, I realize that my upbringing instilled in me a strong inclination toward logic and analysis. Whether for better or worse, this has defined who I am. I've become more analytical than emotional, and I'd readily admit that I'm not a romantic person. Perhaps this analytical mindset acts as a barrier to romance, as I often approach situations with logic and reasonable perspective that doesn't always align with the spontaneity and passion of romance. It might even explain why I never had a serious girlfriend. Yet, it's this same mindset that has driven my growth, allowing me to navigate life with a clear and structured approach.

Again, going back to the Rs 550 purchase of my bicycle, one thing my mother often said still resonates with me. It was a Hindi proverb: '*Apne pair utane hee phailao jitanee chaadar ho*,' which translates to, 'Spread your legs only as far as the bedsheet allows.' In English, this aligns closely with the saying, 'Don't bite off more than you can chew.'

As a child, hearing this repeated proverb felt exhausting, even frustrating at times. I sometimes perceived it as an excuse to avoid fulfilling desires or needs. However, looking back, it makes so much more sense now.

During those days in India, credit cards were virtually nonexistent, and securing a home or car loan was a cumbersome process. Financial management wasn't just a skill; it was a necessity. My parents had to prioritize and plan carefully to ensure stability, and the wisdom in that approach has become clearer with time.

Another common practice during those times was borrowing money among friends. This wasn't limited to teenagers but extended to adults as well. Even my father occasionally borrowed money when there was a genuine need. However, these exchanges were rooted in a close-knit network, built on mutual understanding and trust. It wasn't transactional in the way modern financial systems often feel. Instead, it created a sense of human connection, a dependency balanced by shared values and mutual respect.

Back then, I thought of borrowing as something negative, a sign of inadequacy or failure. But now, I see it differently. Those informal agreements reflected community and empathy. They were a way for people to support one another, bridging gaps in a time when formal financial structures were limited. In hindsight, they represent a beautiful example of human connection, a bond that brought people together to share both burdens and triumphs.

When I compare this to today's world of credit cards and impersonal financial transactions, the contrast is striking. While credit cards offer convenience and the illusion of limitless spending, they often come with high interest rates and the pressure of debt accumulation. The personal touch of borrowing from a friend or family member has been replaced by automated systems, where trust and relationships play no role. The mutual dependency and shared values that defined those older times nurtured not just individuals but entire local communities.

In many ways, that system was better for the local economy and the country. Borrowing among friends and within the community ensured that money stayed within a trusted circle, fostering local economic resilience. It strengthened bonds and encouraged accountability because people knew they were dealing with someone they cared about. Today, the anonymity of modern financial systems can create a sense of detachment, often leading to overextension and financial strain. Reflecting on the simplicity and humanity of those times, I can't help but feel that we lost something valuable in the transition to today's credit-driven world.

One of many lessons etched in my memory revolves around eating the last piece of any good food. I've always had a soft spot for sweets and desserts. Once, there was a box of 'Anarsa' at home—an Indian sweet made with *khoya*, a type of dried milk. Deep-fried and soaked in sweet syrup, it's somewhat akin to a donut—but with a distinct flavor and texture, coated in syrup instead of sugar.

I would occasionally sneak pieces from the box, enjoying them one by one until, finally, I ate the last one. Instead of discarding the empty box, I left it in the refrigerator, pretending it still contained more. That day my mother, unaware, assumed the box still held some Anarsa. When a guest visiting from another city came to our home, she offered to serve him this local delicacy. Anarsa was famous in our hometown, Gaya, and during that time, it wasn't easily available outside our city. Without checking the box, she assured the guest she'd bring him some.

To her surprise, when she opened the box, it was empty. She instantly knew I was the culprit, guilty of eating the last piece and leaving the empty box behind. From another room, I nervously peeped to see how she handled the situation.

With a calm but clearly frustrated tone, she sighed softly and said, "I wish you had just told me instead of setting me up like this." Then, gathering herself, she gracefully apologized to the guest, explaining that the Anarsa was finished but kindly offered to prepare some fresh fritters instead. This, of course, added more work to her already busy day.

The incident left a lasting impression on me. I knew a moral lesson was coming, and it did- never set false expectations, and if you finish something, take responsibility to bring it to its rightful conclusion. Reflecting on this now, I see how it ties into broader principles of economics and resource management. In economics, there is an emphasis on managing finite resources and avoiding the creation of unrealistic expectations. Whether it's a sweet treat or a national budget, the principle remains the same—be honest about what's available and avoid promising what cannot be delivered.

This small incident taught me a profound lesson about accountability and integrity. False hope, whether in personal relationships or economic practices, can lead to disappointment and unnecessary work. By managing expectations and taking responsibility for our actions, we not only respect others but also contribute to a more stable and trustworthy environment. My mother's reaction, calm, resourceful, and constructive, became a model for me to emulate in life and work and till date I don't eat the last piece of any desserts.

Just-in-Time (JIT), a Japanese concept revolutionizing supply chain management, was famously introduced by Toyota to optimize inventory and reduce waste. It emphasizes minimizing excess stock, which is often a liability to an organization. I first encountered this concept during my professional career, but reflecting on my upbringing, I realize that my mother, and many homemakers of the 80s and 90s in India and other developing countries, were natural champions of this philosophy, long before it became a corporate buzzword.

In our household, the refrigerator was not a storage unit for fresh produce or leftovers. It was reserved for essentials like cold water, butter, and occasional sweets. Our meals were typically Indian, revolving around staples like rice or roti, lentils, and green vegetable curries. Meat was a weekly indulgence, usually chicken, fish, or mutton curry, prepared on a Wednesday or Sunday. For the rest of the week, our meals depended entirely on what fresh vegetables the street hawker brought to our doorstep each morning. These vegetables weren't from cold storage but were freshly harvested from nearby villages.

My mother didn't plan meals in advance. Her menu was dictated by the day's fresh arrivals, a true embodiment of the JIT philosophy. Once, I requested my favorite stir-fry with peas, carrots, and cabbage. It remains my favorite to this day, though no version has ever matched the one my mother used to make. Her response to my request was a simple– 'It depends,' a phrase that has now become a hallmark of corporate ambiguity. Her 'it depends' meant that it all hinged on what the street hawker brought that day. Unfortunately for me, peas or carrots were missing that morning, leaving my request unfulfilled.

Disappointed but curious, I asked my mother why we couldn't have a more predictable system. She promised to show me how the entire process worked on her next trip to the downtown market. Unlike the daily visits from the street hawker, the downtown market offered a wider variety of produce at slightly lower prices, though it wasn't practical for daily trips due to the distance from our home. Our reliance on the street hawker, however, was rooted in efficiency. While the hawkers didn't carry staples like potatoes or onions, which are long-lasting and don't require refrigeration, they specialized in fresh greens that needed to be consumed promptly.

On that trip to the downtown market, my mother gave me a crash course in local economics. She showed me how the fresh produce arrived early every morning, direct from nearby villages, and how the sellers engaged in bidding to secure their stock. These small vendors would then distribute the produce to street hawkers who, in turn, brought it to neighborhoods like ours. She explained how proximity played a key role in this system: villages closer to the city focused on cultivating perishable greens, while those further away produced grains and other non-perishables that didn't require daily transportation.

This intricate network of supply and demand operated seamlessly without the need for cold storage or extensive planning, relying instead on trust, timing, and mutual dependence. It struck me how this system not only ensured freshness but also supported local economies, creating a sustainable loop where resources were efficiently managed. Reflecting now, I see the brilliance in this setup. It avoided false expectations, as no one promised what couldn't be delivered. It also aligned perfectly with fundamental economic principles: optimizing limited resources and adapting to what's available, rather than chasing what isn't.

When we were growing up in India, brands like Lux, Surf, and Vim weren't just products, they were synonymous with their categories. Lux wasn't just body soap; it was *the* body soap. Surf wasn't just a detergent powder; it represented the idea of laundry itself. And Vim was the go-to name for dishwashing liquid. I don't recall anyone in our household ever saying– 'The body soap is over,' instead, it was always, 'We need a new Lux.'

Looking back, it wasn't that alternatives didn't exist. There were plenty of options. But for my mom, her philosophy was simple: all these products are essentially the same. To her, there was no point in overthinking it or spending extra money just for a different name. Her practicality shaped the way our household functioned, as time and money were resources to be managed wisely.

Today, in a world driven by branding and consumerism, I often think about how her no-nonsense approach contrasts with modern habits. Now, people deliberate over which soap has the right pH balance, or which detergent is *eco-friendly*. Influencers and ads have turned these basic choices into lifestyle statements. Yet, my mom's voice echoes in my mind– Why waste time or money on what's essentially the same?

It's a lesson that feels especially relevant in an age of overwhelming options, reminding me to step back, prioritize what truly matters, and not get lost in the noise.

Homemakers like my mother were the unsung custodians of this system, demonstrating a resourcefulness that not only kept households running smoothly but also contributed to the resilience of the local economy. Their practices fostered community reliance, reduced waste, and ensured that everyone operated within their means. Unlike today's credit-driven consumerism, where the convenience of credit cards often leads to overspending and unnecessary debt, the systems of the past encouraged thoughtful consumption and financial prudence. This approach not only nurtured local producers but also created a sense of accountability and mutual trust.

My mother's ability to navigate this system and her reliance on 'it depends' taught me valuable lessons about flexibility, resourcefulness, and the importance of living within one's means. It also instilled in me the value of setting realistic expectations, a principle that echoes through both personal choices and economic models. The simplicity of her approach resonates even today, a testament to the timeless wisdom embedded in everyday practices.

In late 2023, Dr. Shefali discussed the concept of becoming 'irrelevant' as parents during an interview with Oprah. She clarified that this doesn't imply parents should disengage from their children's lives. Instead, it highlights the goal of raising children to be independent, empowered, and capable of navigating life's challenges on their own.

According to Dr. Shefali, this requires parents to resist the urge to constantly intervene and instead foster an environment where their children can develop inner strength and resilience. She acknowledged how difficult this can be for parents, as it often feels like a loss of significance in their child's life. However, she emphasized that true parental love lies in nurturing self-sufficient individuals who can confidently find their own way in the world.

Listening to this interview with Dr. Shefali struck a chord with me and gave me the perfect term to describe my mom's parenting style. Her approach was built on similar principles long before I could articulate them or even understand their value. Hearing this discussion made me nostalgic, pulling me back to my first visit home to India from the U.S. in 2008.

I had moved to the U.S. in 2007 for work, and by the fall of 2008, I was returning to India for the first time. During that visit, I made a significant life decision– I bought an apartment in the Delhi NCR region. By then, I was six years into my professional career and felt it was the right time to invest in my own home. Though I was living in the U.S., my initial plan was to work abroad for a while and then return to India, a plan that, to this day, remains unfulfilled.

The apartment was under construction, and I booked it with a mix of personal savings and a bank loan. The decision was made with my wife, Shilpi, and we relied on some local connections in Delhi to finalize the deal. After booking the apartment, I called my mom to share the news. She was thrilled to hear about this milestone, expressing her happiness for my progress. Yet, beneath her words, I sensed a tinge of disappointment. It felt as though she was hurt that such a major decision had been made without involving her or my father.

I didn't press her during that initial conversation, choosing instead to wait until I could speak with her in person. Later, when I visited my hometown and had a moment alone with her, I finally asked, "Aren't you happy that I booked an apartment on my own?"

Her response, though calm, left a lasting impression. She said, "Now you are grown up," and then added something that puzzled me, "You're like a new droplet."

Confused, I asked, "What do you mean?"

She smiled gently and said, "It means you're independent now."

The 'splitting of droplets and forming another' is a fitting analogy for how children grow and eventually make their own start in life. Just as a droplet divides under external forces, children move away from the comfort and support of their parents as they encounter life's pressures and opportunities. Factors like upbringing (fluid properties), life experiences (flow rate), and personal circumstances (channel geometry) shape how they adapt and establish their individuality. Parents, like the original droplet, serve as the foundation, while children carry forward their essence as they create their own paths.

Her words stung. I felt a mix of guilt and sadness, and I couldn't help but ask, "Why would you say that? How can you feel like you don't matter?"

She explained with quiet wisdom that has stayed with me ever since. "When a child starts making decisions on their own," she said, "it is a sign that the parenting was good, that the child is independent and capable. That's what we wanted for you. But it's natural for us to feel like we've taken a step back. It doesn't mean we're not happy, it means we've done our job."

Her explanation mirrored what Dr. Shefali later articulated in her podcast. My mother understood that the ultimate goal of parenting wasn't control or constant involvement but the creation of a strong, self-reliant individual. She embraced this transition, even if it meant feeling 'irrelevant' at times.

Reflecting on it now, I realize how selfless and forward-thinking her approach was. She celebrated my independence, even as it symbolized her stepping back from the center of my life, a testament to her quiet strength and unwavering love.

Lessons From Nurture The Resources: Insights For The Corporate World

- **Empowerment Through Trust**
  Like parents trusting their children to make their own decisions, leaders should empower employees by delegating responsibilities and trusting their judgment. Micromanagement stifles growth, while trust fosters independence and confidence.

- **Independence As Success**
  Just as parents feel a mix of pride and loss when their children become self-reliant, organizations should view employee independence as a success. A team that

can function effectively without constant supervision reflects strong leadership and good systems.

- **Focus On Long-term Growth**
  Parenting aims to prepare children for life's challenges. Similarly, leaders should invest in long-term employee development, equipping their teams with skills and resilience to adapt to change and overcome obstacles.

- **Manage Resources Wisely**
  Just as mother carefully managed resources at home, businesses too must optimize theirs–avoiding overextension while maintaining efficiency. This principle applies to time, money, and manpower.

- **Avoid Creating False Expectations**
  The lesson of not setting false hopes applies directly to client and stakeholder management. Delivering on promises consistently and managing expectations responsibly fosters trust and long-term relationships.

- **Nurture Resilience Through Adversity**
  Parents allow children to face challenges to build resilience. Similarly, leaders should let their teams navigate difficulties and learn

from failures. Protecting them from every challenge may hinder their growth.

- **Celebrate Milestones, But Stay Connected**
  While celebrating individual and team successes is vital, it's equally important to stay connected. Just as one's mother feels a sense of distance when not consulted on major decisions, leaders should remain approachable and encouraging even as their teams grow more independent.

- **Adaptability Over Rigidity**
  Mom's 'it depends' approach exemplifies the value of flexibility in decision-making. In a corporate setting, adaptability to changing circumstances ensures resilience and relevance in dynamic markets.

- **Let Go To Grow**
  The ultimate goal of parenting is to create self-reliant individuals. Similarly, leaders must learn to step back, allowing their teams to take ownership of projects and evolve into future leaders themselves.

- **Celebrate Quiet Leadership**
  Mom's understated yet impactful approach to guiding you aligns with the concept of servant leadership. Leading from behind, with a focus on enabling others to succeed,

creates a culture of mutual respect and sustainable growth.

I wish I had taken the time to truly listen to my mom and cherish her wisdom while I had the chance.

Your Notes: Reflections on Your Own Experience with Parents.

Chapter VI
A Nurse

"Nurses dispense comfort, compassion, and caring without even a prescription."

– Val Saintsbury

Helping those in need, especially during a health crisis, was second nature to my mom. She was always there, calm, steady, and ready to step in when others hesitated. It wasn't just a sense of duty; it was as though compassion flowed through her veins, perhaps inherited from her father, an accomplished physician who had passed away when she was still a teenager. Even without formal medical training, she had an uncanny ability to assess situations, comfort those in distress, and take decisive action when it mattered most.

One moment that truly exemplifies her selflessness involved a distant relative of ours.

Though not very close, our families shared a warm relationship with him. He was a physician himself and had recently celebrated the birth of a baby boy. But joy quickly turned into tragedy when complications during delivery claimed the mother's life, leaving behind a fragile newborn with multiple medical issues.

At the time, our town's healthcare infrastructure was basic at best, and the nearest advanced medical facility was 100 kilometers away. The journey to this hospital wasn't easy, rough, uneven roads stretched endlessly, making travel exhausting and perilous, especially for someone as delicate as the baby. The situation demanded someone who could not only endure the physical challenges of the trip but also take responsibility for the infant's care along the way, feeding him, monitoring his condition, and keeping him safe.

While others debated what to do, my mom stepped forward without hesitation. Cradling the newborn in her arms, she took on the responsibility of his survival during that difficult journey. Her courage and composure in such a heartbreaking situation left a lasting impression on everyone around her. In that moment, she wasn't just a mother or a family member, she became a lifeline, embodying the spirit of a collaborator who offers strength and hope in the darkest of times.

My mom's approach to upskilling me was vastly different from my father's. As a professor, my father was formal, strict, and transactional in his teaching style. Lessons with him often felt like structured tasks with clear objectives. My mother, on the other hand, had a more intuitive and subtle way of teaching me, one that left a profound impact on who I am today.

I can confidently say I'm a pretty good cook and a thoughtful caretaker, and I owe that entirely to my mom. She didn't sit me down for formal cooking lessons, nor did she teach in a conventional step-by-step manner. Her method was more of an 'induction' style, as I described in a prior chapter, learning by observing and doing. I picked up her skills simply by being at her side in the kitchen, watching her magic with ingredients, and lending a hand when needed.

This became especially prominent when my elder sister got married, and my younger sister was pursuing her undergraduate degree at the University of Delhi, 1,000 kilometers from our hometown. With fewer hands at home, my mom would often ask me to join her in the kitchen. At the time, I thought she needed my help, but looking back, I realized her real motive was different. She wanted me to learn, quietly, steadily, how to cook, how to manage a household, and how to be self-reliant.

One day, during one of our conversations, she made a point that she stayed with me. "You'll have to do cooking, whether you like it or not," she said matter-of-factly. To emphasize her point, she used an example that hit close to home: "See your father? He doesn't cook. He can't even make a cup of tea, and that's not good."

Being young and brash, I challenged her logic. "If my father doesn't cook, why should I?" I replied.

I still remember the look on her face, not just anger, but disappointment mingled with determination. She didn't react aggressively or lose her temper. Instead, she patiently explained something that has shaped my perspective on work and fairness ever since.

"It's a different era now," she said firmly. "Moving forward, a better society is one where we don't divide work by gender. Cooking, cleaning, and caring for the home shouldn't be a woman's job or a man's job. These are duties and responsibilities we share as human beings, regardless of gender."

Her words stayed with me, even if I didn't fully appreciate them at the time. Through her example, she taught me that real progress isn't just about technological advancements or financial growth.

It's about evolving how we think, breaking down barriers, and building a society where duties and responsibilities are shared fairly. Her way of teaching wasn't just about cooking, it was about shaping a mindset of equality and mutual respect.

Every morning on my way to the office, I called my mom. It was our ritual, a moment of connection in the midst of busy lives. This time, I asked her for the recipe for 'matar' (sweet pea) curry. As usual, she walked me through the steps, her voice warm and reassuring. Somewhere in the conversation, I blurted out, "I'm tired. It feels like all I do is work, come home, and then go straight into the duty of making food."

Her response caught me off guard. "I am proud of you."

"Proud? What did I do to make you proud?" I asked, genuinely puzzled.

"Because you don't just fulfill duties. You take on responsibilities," she said with a certainty that only a mother could have.

Still confused, I pressed further. "What's the difference?"

She paused, then explained in her usual simple yet profound way. "It's your duty to make sure there's food at home. But it's your responsibility to ensure your wife and kids eat that food and stay healthy."

I frowned. "Aren't they the same thing?"

"No," she said firmly. "Think about it."

Her words stayed with me all day. Even as I prepared dinner that evening and later lay in bed, the distinction between duty and responsibility gnawed at me.

Whenever I felt stuck or confused, I turned to two sources for clarity: my mom and the timeless wisdom of the *Bhagavad Gita*. While I don't consider myself religious, I do see myself as spiritual. The difference between the two? That's a discussion for another chapter.

That night, I flipped through the Gita, searching for insights on duty. The index pointed to over 30 references, but one verse stood out: Chapter 3, Verse 18:

नैव तस्य कृतेनार्थो नाकृतेनेह कश्चन |

न चास्य सर्वभूतेषु कश्चिदर्थव्यपाश्रय: || 18||

naiva tasya kṛitenārtho nākṛiteneha kaścana na
chāsya sarva-bhūteṣhu kaścid artha-vyapāśrayaḥ

Translation: "Such self-realized souls have nothing to gain or lose either in discharging or renouncing their duties. Nor do they need to depend on other living beings to fulfill their self-interest."

I interpreted the verse as presenting two approaches to fulfilling one's duties to the supreme. The first is the path of Karm Yogis, those who perform their worldly duties with devotion and detachment, offering the fruits of their actions to a higher purpose. They balance spiritual growth with practical life, working selflessly without attachment to outcomes. The second path is that of Karm Sanyāsīs, those who renounce all worldly duties to focus entirely on spiritual practices and devotion to God, seeking liberation from material pursuits.

Reading this brought me clarity and satisfaction. It also deepened my curiosity about responsibility, a term I couldn't find in the Gita's index. Being from Gaya, Bihar, just 15 kilometers from Bodh Gaya, where Buddha attained enlightenment, I decided to explore Buddha's teachings on the subject.

Buddha's views on responsibility fascinated me. His teachings emphasize self-reliance, ethical living, and mindfulness. The Dhammapada reminds us that individuals are accountable for their actions, shaping their future through the law of karma. The Noble Eightfold Path, especially Right Action

(Dhammacakkappavattana Sutta), underscores the responsibility to act ethically and avoid harm.

Through dependent origination (Mahanidana Sutta), Buddha illustrates how our actions affect others, highlighting the interconnectedness of life. Teachings on compassion (Metta Sutta) and mindfulness (Satipatthana Sutta) guide us toward reducing harm and fostering harmony.

Lastly, Buddha's focus on acknowledging mistakes and striving for self-improvement (Majjhima Nikaya) frames responsibility as a journey of growth and balance.

The more I delved into the teachings, the more my understanding of responsibility deepened. Excited, I couldn't wait to share my insights with my mom during our next call. When I did, she listened patiently before adding her wisdom–

"Consider your work and family bonds as your duties. But nurturing your children and helping them grow into good humans that's your responsibility. When they're adults, your duty shifts to letting go of worldly needs and focusing on your spiritual growth. That, too, is a responsibility, to yourself."

Her words left me pondering. Even today, I'm still trying to fully understand their depth, but they remain a guiding light in my life.

August 2012, New York City was abuzz with an unusual celebration of equality, the right to bare chests. On a hot and humid Sunday, about two dozen topless women gathered in a park to protest what they called 'National Go-Topless Day,' drawing attention to the disparity in topless rights between men and women. The protest made headlines, and like many others at the time, I came across it in a physical newspaper. Yes, the tangible, ink-smudged pages of a newspaper, a relic I still enjoyed more than its digital counterpart.

The next day, during my routine call with Mom, she asked her usual question, "What's new in the U.S.?"

I hesitated, then laughed as I recounted the story of the topless protest in New York. For a moment, there was silence on the other end. I thought perhaps the connection had dropped or that the topic had made her uncomfortable. But then she replied, her voice steady and thoughtful:

"That's the fundamental problem these days. Women are trying to copy what men are doing, but that's not necessary. If women truly want equality, they should advocate for men to uphold higher standards, not lower themselves to match what men do. Women should lead by uplifting the standard, not just mimicking it."

Her response struck me. It wasn't just about clothing or protests; it was a profound commentary on how societal progress should aim for elevation, not imitation. By the time our conversation ended and I reached the office, her words stayed with me, sparking deeper reflection.

One of the thoughts that followed was about cheerleading in American high school football. I couldn't help but draw a parallel between the topless protest and the traditional roles assigned to women in sports culture.

Cheerleading, especially at high school football games, is still predominantly female. While I'm aware that boys can be cheerleaders too, the activity remains overwhelmingly girl-dominated.

Why do we still have girls performing as cheerleaders at football matches?

Sure, cheerleading has evolved into a sport of its own, requiring athleticism and skill. But in the context of football, it often feels like a relic of a bygone era. Shouldn't we move beyond these roles that subtly reinforce traditional expectations of women as supporters and entertainers rather than equals on the field?

The protest and my mom's perspective gave me much to ponder. Perhaps the real challenge lies in reimagining equality, not as a race to mimic one another but as a shared responsibility to redefine societal norms for the better. Women and men both have the power to challenge and uplift these standards, starting with the smallest, most overlooked traditions.

The next call with my mom began with a thought-provoking question from her, "Do you realize why I made sure you learned to cook?"

I replied, "Yes, so I can help with household chores."

She agreed but quickly added, "That's not the only reason. The main reason is that cooking isn't just a woman's task; it's everyone's responsibility in a home. If society expects everyone to work and earn regardless of gender, shouldn't household chores follow the same principle?"

Her words stayed with me. That day, I promised myself to raise my kids, regardless of gender, to know how to cook and take care of household tasks, rejecting any notion that certain chores are gender-specific.

But then, she surprised me by saying, "We still have duties influenced by gender."

Confused, I asked, "What do you mean?"

"If circumstances allow," she explained, "women should take charge of the kitchen."

Her statement left me stunned. "Mom, that sounds contradictory! You can't argue for equality and then say this."

She responded calmly. "It's not a contradiction. Life isn't always binary. Women often have a natural compassion and empathy that make them particularly suited to nurturing roles, like feeding the family."

I didn't have a quick rebuttal, so I just listened.

Her words left me curious, so later that evening, I did some research. I found an article on JSTOR titled– 'Is Empathy Gendered and, If so, Why?' by Claudia Strauss. Is Empathy Gendered and, If so, Why? An Approach from Feminist Psychological Anthropology Claudia Strauss Ethos Vol. 32, No. 4, Theme Issue: Contributions to a Feminist Psychological Anthropology (Dec., 2004), pp. 432-457 (26 pages). It explored how empathy might be linked to gender roles and societal expectations. Surprisingly, it aligned with some of what my mom had said.

The next day, I called her back and shared my findings.

She listened quietly and then said, "Good. But let me ask you this: why do you think so many professionally educated, working women shy away from cooking and managing the kitchen these days?"

I had been thinking about this too. "Honestly, Mom, it's not entirely their fault. If anyone's to blame, it's their parents. Both moms and dads need to teach their kids the value of these skills, regardless of gender."

To my surprise, she agreed wholeheartedly. "You're absolutely right," she said.

That call left me energized and thoughtful. It's incredible how a conversation with my mom can open my mind to new perspectives and leave me motivated for the day ahead.

In another conversation with my mom, the topic of duty and responsibilities resurfaced. This time, I mentioned a thought that had been on my mind:

"People who were teenagers in the 90s have witnessed the most significant changes, especially in India. The shift from a closed to an open economy, the rise of technology, and so much more."

My mom's reply was immediate, "Every generation says the same about their time."

Not one to back down, I countered, "True, but our generation is unique. We spent the first half of our lives afraid of our parents, especially our fathers, and now, in the second half, we're afraid of our kids. And somewhere in between, the men are also afraid of their wives."

Mom paused, clearly reflecting on my comment, and then said, "You're not entirely wrong. Your generation is indeed sandwiched between duty and responsibility, all while trying to find balance."

Her words stayed with me.

The idea of being 'sandwiched' perfectly described the constant juggling act of my generation. We are navigating the traditional expectations of respecting and caring for our parents while also adapting to modern demands, raising children with different values and priorities. And through it all, there's an internal struggle to fulfill our responsibilities while not losing ourselves in the process.

This conversation lingered in my mind long after it ended. It made me think about how every generation faces its unique challenges, but ours seems to bear the weight of bridging two very different worlds. The changes we've seen, cultural, technological, and economic, have shaped not just the way we live, but the way we think about our roles within family and society.

Mom's observation about our search for balance hit a nerve. It wasn't just about duty or responsibility anymore; it was about finding a way to integrate the two without losing our sense of purpose. And perhaps, that's the real challenge of our time.

While pursuing my degree from the Business School at the University of Minnesota, I had the privilege to take a course titled 'Competing Globally' by Svjetlana Madzar. It was a transformative experience, one where I excelled academically but also found myself increasingly drawn into conversations with my mom that mirrored the very themes we discussed in class. These discussions often left me reflecting on the cultural complexities I navigate daily, particularly being someone who grew up in India but now works and lives in the United States.

One of the topics that triggered a long and thought-provoking conversation was the cultural orientation towards time. People from the United States have a strong future orientation. They plan, innovate, and make decisions with a focus on what lies ahead, often disregarding the past unless it holds direct value for the future. In contrast, in India, the cultural orientation leans heavily toward the past. History, traditions, and experiences are viewed as foundational to decision-making. This contrast manifests in various ways, including business practices– while Americans emphasize research and innovation, Indians often draw on past successes as evidence of future potential.

When I shared this with my mom, she listened attentively, and her response was both insightful and challenging. She said, "Every generation believes their time is unique, but what makes yours different is that you're living in a world where the past and future constantly clash."

She wasn't wrong. Growing up in India, where traditions and historical context shaped much of my worldview, and now working in the United States, where the focus is forward-looking and individualistic, it often leaves me feeling caught in the middle. Am I clinging too much to the past, or am I losing sight of it entirely in trying to adapt to the future-focused mindset of the U.S.?

Another conversation revolved around the concept of individualism versus collectivism. The United States values individualism, decisions are made independently, personal freedom is prioritized, and success is often seen as a singular achievement.

India, on the other hand, emphasizes community and group orientation. Decisions are made collectively, and the welfare of the group often takes precedence over personal ambition. My professor highlighted how these differences influence workplace dynamics. In the U.S., quick decision-making and direct communication are common, while in India, consultation, consensus, and group harmony are valued.

When I discussed this with my mom, it sparked a deeper exploration of my own identity.

"You're working in an individualistic culture," she said, "but you were raised in a collectivist one. It's no wonder you feel torn." Her words resonated deeply.

At work, I often find myself trying to balance assertiveness with empathy, directness with inclusivity. It's a constant tug-of-war between two cultural paradigms, and more often than not, I feel stuck in the middle, struggling to reconcile these differing values.

These cultural intersections have shaped my worldview but also left me in a state of perpetual negotiation. Navigating these differences isn't just a professional challenge; it's a deeply personal one.

As someone who straddles these two worlds, I've realized that understanding and embracing these cultural dimensions is not about choosing one over the other but finding a way to bridge the gap, a journey I'm still on.

It was the summer of 2012, a special time for me–I was celebrating my son's first birthday. Our home was filled with laughter, decorations, and the warmth of family. An extended family member was also visiting us, making the occasion even livelier. In the midst of the celebrations, I found myself on a morning call with my mom, sharing details of the gathering.

As we talked, she suddenly said, "Guest or host are like liquid."

I laughed. "What does that even mean?"

She chuckled. "Think about it. Liquid takes the shape of its container, right? A good guest or host should do the same. A host should make their guest feel comfortable, and a guest should blend in, adapting to the space rather than resisting it like a solid."

I nodded, intrigued. "So, you're saying hospitality should be effortless, like how liquid flows into spaces naturally?"

"Exactly," she said. "A good host doesn't force things; they create an environment where everything moves smoothly. And guests, well, they shouldn't be rigid like a solid–if they are too fixed in their ways, they create tension, and things break. On the other hand, if they are like gas–too scattered, without boundaries or presence–then they evaporate, and their presence doesn't leave any lasting connection."

"That makes sense," I admitted. "But doesn't liquid also mix with whatever it touches?"

"Ah," she said, "and that's the beauty of it. A guest and a host influence each other. The host sets the atmosphere, but the guest's attitude shapes the experience too. Unlike gas, which spreads without boundaries, or a solid, which resists change, liquid adapts—it balances, connects, and leaves an impression without overwhelming."

I smiled, letting the thought sink in. "And just like liquid doesn't stay in one place forever, the roles of guest and host are temporary."

"Yes," she agreed. "People come and go, but the impact of their presence can last much longer."

As I hung up the phone, I looked around at the bustling house. In that moment, I realized—whether in homes, workplaces, or fleeting encounters, we are all sometimes the guest and sometimes the host. And the way we flow into each other's lives matters more than we think.

Insights For The Corporate World

Lessons From Nurses In The Corporate World

- **Empathy And Compassion**: Like nurses, leaders should understand team members' needs, provide support, and foster a caring work environment. Compassionate leadership improves morale and loyalty.

- **Calm Under Pressure**: Nurses excel in managing crises with composure. Similarly, corporate leaders should remain steady during challenges, offering clear guidance and support to their teams.
- **Strengthen Team Dynamics**: Use individual rewards for motivation in individualistic cultures. In collectivist cultures, implement group-oriented incentives to boost team morale and cohesion.

Duty vs. Responsibility In The Corporate Context

- **Understand The Difference**: Duty is fulfilling assigned tasks (e.g., meeting deadlines, adhering to policies), while responsibility is owning the outcomes (e.g., ensuring the team delivers quality work). Encourage employees to go beyond duties and take responsibility for results.
- **Cultivate Ownership**: Create a workplace culture where employees feel accountable not just for their roles but for the broader impact of their work on the team and organization.
- **Balance Task And Impact**: Managers should emphasize that it's not just about completing tasks (duty) but ensuring they

contribute positively to the overall goals (responsibility).

- **Leadership Example**: Leaders should model responsibility by addressing issues proactively, showing that they are not just fulfilling duties but also ensuring success for the entire team.
- **Develop Self-Reflection**: Use feedback and mentorship to help employees reflect on the difference between what they are required to do and what they can do to create a positive difference.

Empathy And Emotional Intelligence

- **Emphasize Empathy In Leadership**: Recognize that compassion and understanding are valued in Indian collectivist cultures. Use these traits to build trust and strong relationships within diverse teams.
- **Create Lasting Relationships**: In collectivist environments, invest time in relationship building to secure long-term partnerships and mutual respect.

I wish I had taken the time to truly listen to my mom and cherish her wisdom while I had the chance.

Your Notes: Reflections on Your Own Experience with Parents.

Chapter VII
The Embodiment Of Tolerance

"Learn the art of balance from the ever-evolving holiness of Mother Nature."

- Pushpa Sinha (My mother)

The bond between Earth and a mother is deeply rooted in the shared role of nurturing and sustaining life. Both are life-givers, tirelessly providing the essential resources for survival and growth. Just as a mother nourishes her children with food, shelter, and care, Earth offers humanity its bounty, food from its soil, water from its rivers, and air to breathe.

Both embody protection: a mother shields her child from harm, while Earth's atmosphere safeguards life from the harshness of space. This shared essence of provision, protection, and interdependence makes the metaphor of 'Mother Earth' resonate universally, serving as a reminder of the profound lessons both can teach about tolerance and coexistence.

My mother at times reminded us, "You will never understand the pain of being a mother." These words stayed with me, sometimes fading into the background but always re-emerging in moments of tension.

One ordinary day, I called her, as I often did, and noticed something different in her voice, it was lower, tinged with exhaustion. Concerned, I asked, "What's wrong?"

She sighed and replied, "Our domestic help took the day off, and now all the chores are on me."

Trying to lighten her burden, I suggested, "Why don't you order food from outside?"

Her response was immediate, almost indignant. "Don't you know your father? He won't eat food from outside."

Without thinking, I retorted, "It's not just him, it's you too who won't eat food from outside."

The moment those words left my mouth, I regretted them. Her irritation was palpable, and I could hear the frustration building. The conversation quickly spiraled. What began as a discussion about the day's inconveniences soon transformed into a deeper emotional outpouring.

"You all will never truly understand," she said, her voice cracking slightly. "It's not just about carrying you for nine months or enduring sleepless nights while raising you. It's the mental toll, the constant struggle to give you all, the best environment to grow and succeed. Every choice I made, every sacrifice, was for you all. But that kind of pain, the kind that comes from wanting so much for your children, you can't possibly comprehend until you've lived it yourselves."

As she spoke, I had already reached the parking ramp of my office. But instead of ending the call, I stayed in the car, parked, and let her continue. I realized that more than anything, she needed someone to listen to. Her voice softened as she shared her struggles, and I could sense a slight ease in her tone. For her, this wasn't just a conversation, it was a moment to vent, to release the weight she carried silently every day.

By the time we ended the call, I felt grateful for the opportunity to truly listen to her. In those few minutes, it felt like I had given her something she often gave us without hesitation, her time, her attention, and her patience. It wasn't much, but I could tell it made a difference, and that small act of listening felt like a quiet gesture of respect that she deserved.

The next day, my call with Mom started on a lighter note. Her tone was cheerful as she mentioned that the domestic help had returned, and she dismissed the previous day's frustration as 'just a bad day.' I smiled, relieved to hear her in better spirits.

As we chatted, I decided to revisit her comment about the nine months of pregnancy.

"Mom," I began, "I agree that a woman becomes a parent before a man does. After all, a woman can feel the child, the fetus, long before the father can. But if that's the case, why is it that a child usually takes the father's last name or family name, not the mother's?"

Her answer was simple and straightforward. "That's just the way it's been for generations," she said.

I was in a teasing mood and decided to push further. "But why, Mom? Why does it have to be that way?"

She chuckled, slightly exasperated, and replied, "Because that's how it works."

Satisfied that the conversation was staying lighthearted, we moved on to other topics. By the time I reached the office, the call had wrapped up normally.

Before diving into what came next, it's worth mentioning a bit about my childhood. Growing up in a joint family, we shared a large house with my father's three brothers. Over time, the family split into four separate apartments within the same house, each with its own kitchen, though we shared a common entry and utilities.

One of my uncles was a botany professor with a passion for research. His 'laboratory' was often our yard, where he and his Ph.D. students conducted experiments on plant mutations, combining eggplants with tomatoes and other creative ventures. He even had a professional-grade microscope at home, which, to us teenagers, was both a curiosity and, admittedly, a toy.

Playing with that microscope, we stumbled into learning—about everything from Watson and Crick's DNA structure to the 23 pairs of chromosomes that make up human genetics. We absorbed knowledge far beyond what most school students our age were exposed to—and it was fun. Those experiments left an indelible mark on my understanding of science and planted a sense of curiosity that still guides me today.

The day after that cheerful call, I spoke to Mom again, thinking the discussion about names was behind us. To my surprise, it wasn't.

"It's the male who determines whether the child will be male or female," she said, picking up right where we left off. "That's the scientific reason."

My mind immediately jumped back to what I'd learned as a teenager–the 23rd pair of chromosomes. I responded, "Ah, I see! The male contributes either an X or Y chromosome, and that's what decides the baby's sex."

She seemed pleased with my understanding but added another layer to the explanation. "Traditionally," she said, "men were the breadwinners in families. Back in those days, most work required physical strength, and men were naturally built for it. That's why the family name and lineage typically followed the father."

Her reasoning blended biology with the social structures of the past–a lens shaped by both evolution and era. But today, that narrative is shifting. In a world where intelligence, emotional insight, and adaptability are equally–if not more–valuable than brute strength, the idea of lineage and leadership being tied to gender feels increasingly outdated.

As the conversation wound down, Mom lightened the mood with a smile in her voice. "But really," she said, quoting Shakespeare, "'What's in a name?'"

That mix of tradition, science, and gentle humor–it was classic Mom. And in her own way, she was inviting me to question, think, and evolve.

We both laughed, and the conversation ended on a note of mutual understanding and humor.

April 2009. It was a life-changing month for us as we welcomed our first child here in the USA. My mother had traveled all the way to be with us for the delivery, offering the kind of support only a mother can provide. The arrival of our baby was filled with excitement, joy, and, of course, the whirlwind of responsibilities that come with being first-time parents. Sleepless nights became our new normal as my wife and I juggled feedings, diaper changes, and soothing a crying infant in the wee hours.

Surprisingly, though, I didn't feel exhausted. I was running on just four or five hours of sleep most nights, yet there was an energy, an inexplicable drive, that kept me going. One day, during a quiet moment, I shared this with my mom.

Sitting across from her, I said, "I'm barely sleeping these days, maybe four or five hours at most, but I don't feel tired. I don't understand how that's even possible."

She listened carefully, her expression a mix of concern and knowing. Her first response was practical. "That's not good," she said gently. "You have to take care of yourself too. Your health is important, for you, for the baby, and for your wife."

But then, as only she could, she offered a deeper insight that struck a chord in my heart.

She smiled softly and said, "Now you'll begin to understand how much I loved you. This realization only comes when you become a parent yourself."

Her words hung in the air, carrying a weight that was both profound and humbling.

She continued, "At times, the pain we endure as parents is overlooked, not because it's our duty or responsibility, but because of love. It's love that gives us the strength to push through exhaustion, to keep going when everything else stops. Love is a power unlike anything else. It can't be defined, nor does it need to be. You just feel it."

Her words stayed with me long after our conversation ended. I began to see my own actions, waking up at odd hours, rocking my child back to sleep, finding joy in the smallest of smiles, in a new light. It wasn't just about fulfilling responsibilities;

it was about the boundless love I now understood more deeply than ever before.

In that moment, I realized that parenting is not just about giving life, it's about living love. My mother's words weren't just a reflection of her experience; they were a gift, a bridge connecting her journey as a parent to mine.

Like many middle-class women, my mother celebrated every festival and ritual with devotion and joy. But among them, there were two rituals that were particularly close to her heart. The first was a monthly fast she observed with unshakable commitment. She would abstain from food and water for an entire day, breaking the fast only after moonrise. The second, and arguably the most significant to her, was *Chhath Puja*, a festival that radiated her unwavering spirituality and respect for nature.

The monthly offering to the moon, or the *Chandra Puja*, was a ritual my mother and one of our aunts performed with unwavering devotion. While we didn't necessarily understand the significance of the ritual, it was clear that it mattered deeply to the adults.

On those evenings, mom and auntie would carry small pots of water, and under the serene glow of the moonlight, they would offer the water with folded hands and quiet prayers. For us kids, it was more of an obligation than an event of interest. The ritual felt repetitive, and on many occasions, we were reluctant participants. But not attending wasn't an option; we were required to be there.

One such evening, when I was likely in the seventh grade, my curiosity finally got the better of me. I turned to my mother and asked, "Why do you do this puja, Mom? What's the point?"

Her answer was as simple as it was profound.

"Why not?" she said, her voice calm but resolute. Sensing my skepticism, she elaborated. "Do you know that the moon's movement affects the tides in the sea? That's scientifically proven, isn't it?" she asked, pausing for a moment to let the question sink in. I nodded hesitantly.

She continued, "Well, think about it, just as the moon influences the vast waters of the ocean, it also has an effect on us. After all, more than 60% of the human body is water. It's only natural that the moon impacts us too. Offering water to the moon during this puja is a way to harmonize with that energy. It's a gesture that fosters balance and positivity."

I wasn't entirely convinced. "But how is that science?" I asked, still trying to grasp the connection.

Her response left a lasting impression on me. “Science,” she said, “is simply the understanding of nature as it truly is. It’s about observing, questioning, and connecting the dots. The rituals we perform may seem like mere traditions, but many of them are rooted in an understanding of nature, an understanding that we, as humans, are still figuring out. Just because we don’t fully understand something yet doesn’t mean it isn’t real or important.”

Her words made me pause. They revealed a depth to these seemingly simple rituals that I hadn’t considered before. For my mother, the puja wasn’t just an act of faith; it was a way of aligning herself with the rhythms of the universe, an acknowledgment of the unseen forces that govern life.

That evening, standing under the moonlit sky, I realized that what I had dismissed as superstition was, for her, a bridge between the spiritual and the scientific. It wasn’t about blind belief, it was about respect for the interconnectedness of all things, a reverence for the mysteries of nature that we are still striving to decode.

Even now, when I think of those rituals, I am reminded of her wisdom. She taught me that faith and science are not necessarily opposites but can coexist as two sides of the same coin.

Her explanations, though simple, held layers of meaning that resonate with me to this day.

Chhath Puja, deeply rooted in the traditions of Bihar, Jharkhand, Uttar Pradesh, and parts of West Bengal of India, is a powerful expression of gratitude to the Sun God (*Surya Dev*) and *Chhathi Maiya*, the goddess of energy. The festival spans four days, with its most rigorous practice being a 36-hour fast observed without food or water. It involves prayers, offerings, and the serene rituals of worshipping the Sun at both sunrise and sunset.

For my mother, this wasn't merely a religious observance—it was a profound reminder of humanity's dependence on nature and the balance required to sustain life on Earth.

Around the time of Chhath Puja, I called my mother. As the festivities carried on back home, I couldn't help but express my feelings.

"I miss the festival so much," I said, my voice tinged with nostalgia.

"I miss you too," she replied warmly. "But it's fine, you're where you need to be."

As our conversation continued, she brought up Chhath Puja in a way that was uniquely her own, equal parts practical and philosophical.

"Chhath is a festival where you see and worship," she explained. "It's not about praying to a God you haven't seen; it's about offering respect and gratitude to something you witness every day–the Sun. It's a reminder of nature's importance and how essential it is to maintain its balance."

Her words carried a wisdom that always left me thinking. In a playful tone, I responded, "So that's why you're such a fan of Chhath Puja, huh?"

She laughed lightly and said, "You can think whatever you like, it's fine."

From there, our conversation drifted toward the Earth and the impact of human actions. My mother's insight was sharp and unflinching.

"We humans need nature, but nature doesn't need us," she said matter-of-factly. "The forests, the animals, the birds, all the other creatures on this Earth, would not only survive but thrive without humans. But we humans can't survive without nature. And yet, we act as if we own it, as if we're separate from it. We're so selfish that we don't even care."

Her words stayed with me long after we ended the call. They weren't just observations; they were truths we often overlook. Through her rituals and the wisdom she shared, my mother taught me lessons that went beyond the surface of tradition and faith. She showed me that festivals like Chhath Puja aren't just about rituals or community–they're a call to recognize the symbiotic relationship between humanity and the natural world.

In her quiet yet resolute way, my mother embodied a reverence for nature that many of us forget in the rush of modern life. She didn't just celebrate the festivals; she lived their essence–gratitude, respect, and the understanding that humanity's survival is deeply intertwined with the balance of the natural world.

That's why I feel so proud today that both of my sisters are carrying her legacy forward. Every year, they observe Chhath Puja with the same devotion and sincerity. Through their actions, the spirit of our mother continues–quiet, steadfast, and rooted in something far greater than ritual alone.

March 2020. The world was gripped by uncertainty as the Covid-19 pandemic began to unfold. Fear and confusion rippled through every corner of the globe, and like everyone else, my mother and I were trying to make sense of it all. Despite the chaos, our daily phone calls remained a comforting ritual.

Mom, as always, was concerned but remarkably optimistic. "This too shall pass," she would say, her voice steady and reassuring.

One day, during one of our conversations, I brought up the enormity of the pandemic. "Why do you think something like this happens, Mom? An epidemic on such a scale?" I asked, hoping she might offer one of her simple yet profound perspectives.

Her response was calm, almost matter-of-fact. "When we go against nature and stop respecting it, nature finds a way to correct the imbalance," she said. "Nature is powerful, far more than we realize. It has its own way of maintaining balance, its own check-and-balance system. And sometimes, that means loss, terrible loss. Thousands may have to give their lives, but it's like nature resetting its parameters."

Her words struck a chord, but I couldn't have imagined just how personal her statement would become. I never thought, not even in my worst nightmares, that I would lose her to this very pandemic. Yet, on September 6, 2020, my world shattered. My mother succumbed to Covid-19.

The loss was devastating. It was more than losing a parent; it was losing a source of wisdom, strength, and unconditional love. I couldn't help but think back to her words during that March call. She had spoken of nature's power, of its ability to restore balance, but I never expected her to become part of that balance, a sacrifice to the reset she had so calmly described.

My Last Conversation With Mom

Our final conversation was brief–"Okay, we'll talk later," she said. It was just a week before September 6, 2020.

At the time, she was in Ranchi with my elder sister, having gone there to stay safe from the rising COVID-19 threat and be with family. Ironically, we believe she may have contracted the virus while distributing blankets to the poor–something she did selflessly, even in uncertain times.

The next day, when I called her, my sister answered. "Mom is in the hospital," she said. I remember feeling strangely calm. I thought to myself, "Good. Now she's under care–she'll be fine." None of us imagined, even for a moment, that she wouldn't return.

But by the fourth day of her hospitalization, she was on a ventilator. We were suddenly consulting multiple physicians, trying to understand her condition through vital signs and reports–grasping at hope, clinging to faith.

On the morning of September 6, at 5:00 AM CST, my phone rang. I was in the U.S. The message on the other end was simple and shattering: **"She is no more."**

In the middle of the global pandemic, with travel restrictions and lockdowns in place, I somehow made it to India to perform her last rites—as her son, and as her student. A mentee saying goodbye to his first and greatest teacher.

In the early days after her passing, I found myself obsessively preserving her belongings—her photos, her clothes, small things she had touched—as if holding on to them would hold on to her. But then, one day, a thought struck me like lightning: **Why am I chasing her memory through objects when I carry her within me?**

I exist because of her. I am her legacy, her reflection. I am not separated from her—not now, not ever. If anything, I feel more connected to her now than I ever did. Not through photographs or heirlooms, but through the values she instilled in me, the conversations we had, and the life I strive to lead.

In the days that followed, I found myself reflecting on the countless lessons she had imparted, especially her reverence for nature. My mother had always believed that humans are merely guests on this Earth, dependent on its resources but far too reckless in our use of them.

She would often remind me, “Nature doesn’t need us. We need nature. And the moment we forget that, we invite our own destruction.”

Even in the pain of her loss, her words carried a profound truth. The pandemic wasn’t just a biological crisis; it was a stark reminder of the fragility of human life and the immense power of nature. Her passing became a turning point for me, deepening my respect for the balance she spoke of and the lessons she tried to teach me.

Now, as I look back on that conversation and the wisdom she shared, I feel a bittersweet gratitude. She left me with a lens through which to see the world, a world she loved deeply, even with all its flaws. And though I’ll always ache for her presence, I carry her voice with me, a reminder of the resilience and grace she embodied, even in the face of nature’s most devastating blows.

Insights For The Corporate World– ‘The Embodiment Of Tolerance’

- **Balance Is Key To Sustainability:** Nature maintains equilibrium to sustain life, demonstrating that long-term success requires balance. In business, sustainability comes from harmonizing profit with ethics, growth with stability, and productivity with employee well-being.

- **Active Listening Fosters Strong Leadership:** Genuine listening strengthens relationships, whether within a family or an organization. Leaders who take the time to understand employees, customers, and stakeholders cultivate trust, engagement, and a more resilient company culture.

- **Adaptability And Resilience Drive Success:** Life presents constant challenges and managing them effectively requires adaptability. Just as a household navigates uncertainties, organizations must stay agile in response to market shifts, technological advancements, and global disruptions.

- **Legacy Is Built Through Values, Not Just Names:**
  Influence and respect are not inherited but earned through values and actions. A family name alone does not create a legacy, just as in business, where corporate culture and ethical leadership hold greater weight than branding or reputation.

- **Interdependence Is The Foundation Of Strength:**
  The natural world thrives on interconnectedness, illustrating that strength comes from collaboration. Businesses and communities succeed when

individuals, teams, and external partners work cohesively toward shared goals.

- **Respecting Tradition And Innovation Equally:**
  Tradition and progress are often seen as opposing forces, yet they can coexist. Faith and science, wisdom and technology, when blended thoughtfully, they drive meaningful evolution, both in personal growth and corporate strategy.

- **Ignoring Nature's Balance Has Consequences:**
  Imbalances in nature correct themselves, often in ways that serve as cautionary lessons. Whether in ecosystems or economies, overexploitation, neglect, or short-term thinking ultimately lead to disruption, reinforcing the importance of sustainable decision-making.

I wish I had taken the time to truly listen to my mom and cherish her wisdom while I had the chance.

Your Notes: Reflections on Your Own Experience with Parents.

Beyond The Horizon

The ancient Greek philosopher Heraclitus once said, "Change is the only constant"—a truth that resonates deeply in the ever-evolving journey of parenthood, or more broadly, in the path of nurturers. Over time, the role of caregiving has transformed—from being seen as primarily a mother's responsibility to becoming a shared, dynamic partnership between mothers, fathers, and caregivers. Yet, even amid this positive evolution, some aspects remain uniquely tied to each parent.

Pregnancy and childbirth, for example, are not simply biological events; they are sacred processes that define a woman's irreplaceable role in the circle of life. Honoring these natural rhythms is essential—not as a rejection of progress or innovation, but as a way to stay connected to what makes us deeply, beautifully human.

My mother's legacy embodies this balance—a profound respect for life's natural cycles alongside a spirit of adaptability and strength. She taught me that while change is inevitable, the core essence of nurturing, love, and respect for nature must remain steadfast. In a world increasingly driven by artificial substitutes and shortcuts, remembering this legacy is more important than ever. For if we lose touch with these fundamental truths, we risk losing not only our connection to nature but also the very essence of who we are.

When searching for books on 'purpose of life,' 'finding your purpose,' 'meaning of life,' 'life purpose,' 'career purpose,' 'spiritual purpose' on Amazon.com, thousands of books appear—each offering a different perspective. This abundance of viewpoints is a testament to the diversity of human experience.

If there were only one singular answer to life's purpose, humanity itself might have stagnated or ceased to exist.

My purpose is uniquely my own, deeply shaped by my mother's influence. In discovering it, I have come to embrace a simple yet fulfilling life—one that seeks to make the world a better place.

Like many, I admire great scholars and intellectuals, and one of my favorite books is Discover

Your True North by Bill George. Reflecting on its teachings alongside my own experiences, I have realized that life should not be compartmentalized into rigid categories. Instead, what truly matters is the flow–the seamless integration of experiences, values, and relationships. Coexistence and balance are the keys to a meaningful life.

Mom, I never said this before, but mummy, I love you so much.

As I reflect on everything you have taught me–about love, respect, resilience, and the fluid nature of life–I realize that your wisdom was a guiding light, even when I didn't fully understand it. Your presence, like a river, shaped my journey in ways I could never measure.

The **Bible** says: *"Honor your father and mother"* (*Ephesians* 6:2), and through your life, you showed me that honoring a parent isn't just about obedience–it's about carrying forward their wisdom, their kindness, and their love in all that we do.

The **Bhagavad Gita** teaches: *"For one who has been honored, dishonor is worse than death."* (Bhagavad Gita 2:34). You showed me that true honor comes not from titles or power, but from how we treat others, how we respect different viewpoints, and how we stand firm in our values without rigidity.

Mummy, your love was never loud, but it was always present. And now, as I put these words on paper, I want you to know–I see it, I feel it, and I will carry it forward.

I love you so much.

Your Notes: Reflections on Your Own Experience with Parents.